LIGHT

THROUGH THE

CRACKS

D1617273

LYDIA DEAN

Light Through The Cracks
Published by Lotus Light Publishing

ISBN: 978-0-9908213-2-8
MEMOIR

QUANTITY PURCHASES: Schools, companies, professional groups, clubs, and other organizations may qualify for special terms when ordering quantities of this title. For information, email Lydia@gophilanthropic.com.

DISCLAIMER
Some names and identifying details have been changed where the subject matter is sensitive and to protect the privacy of individuals and organizations.

DEDICATION

THANK YOU TO THE POWERFUL influences in my life—the combination of truth seekers and compassionate light workers who have journeyed before me and those I am blessed to walk next to each day. They have taught me my most valuable lessons and have inspired me to work on behalf of a much greater whole.

I want to thank my incredible family, who offers an endless source of love. You've been my cheerleaders and my critics, both of which were essential to complete this book. Thank you to my husband who, since the age of fifteen, has carefully protected the space that has allowed me to discover who I am. He has also made sure I laughed—a lot—along the way.

Last but not least, thank you to Mother Nature, who shows us that harmony and perfection already exist within us, and for the unseen Spirit world that provides us the signs we need to be on our best path.

In order to help others find their greatness, we must continue to find our own.

INTRODUCTION

I WAS SURE AFTER I PUBLISHED *Jumping the Picket Fence* that it would be my only book. But life has a funny way of letting us know we aren't in the lead. As the events unfolded after the publishing of that book, I knew in my heart that I needed to document them. And when I had done so, I could begin the process of understanding.

In putting these chapters together, it was my hope to make sense of the hidden messages and lessons embedded in the events of life, to see the meaning of the painting that had already been painted. For me, the process of writing has helped me piece together the interconnection of things, as opposed to accepting the one dimension of the moment. While digging through the memories and finding the words that applied to them, I was forced to look again, to discern what might be lying below the surface.

Throughout the pages, I hope to give credit to those who have helped me see the beauty that emerges from a search for truth and justice in the world—for we are not a simple product of our experience, of our own making. We carry with us the wisdom, the pain, and the dreams of those who have been on the path before us. They have laid the foundation for what we need to carry on.

This book brings forth themes that continue to inspire intro-spection in myself and the world around me—a profound desire to contribute value to humanity—and a search for my true home. It also reflects a coursework in life that forced me to acknowledge the importance of giving to myself as a vital, essential part of being able to give to others; healing the world begins within ourselves.

PROLOGUE

The only true gift is a portion of thyself.

— Ralph Waldo Emerson

I WOULD STARE INTO THE DEPTHS of her black eyes, which I was sure went into the very soul of the earth. I was also convinced they touched the clouds, where the spirit world communicated directly through her. Tauheedah is a shamanic healer in the San Fernando Valley of Los Angeles. There is something larger than life about her, a reminder to not take what we see at face value because there might be way more to it than meets the eye. I had started seeing her a few months before, not long after moving out to the West Coast from Rochester, New York, for our teenage son Nick's developing music career. I had a growing intrigue for the mystical world—a curious interest for what wasn't falling into neat logical boxes, which seemed to be everything at the time. I understood that there was more to life than what we could see—as if other powers were navigating the whole scene behind a veil, making sure it would all end up as it was meant to be.

Tauheedah doesn't ask questions. She just seems to know what is going on inside of you—and all around you. Instead of feeling like you are drowning in your worries, she has you moving through them, swimming through them, as though you are gracefully observing your life as a calm and unbiased outsider. She talks of strange past lives, weaving them into the present like there is nothing odd about it—like we can all see as she does. My sessions with her felt indulgent at first, like I didn't deserve this attention. But once stretched out on the table in her cool, dark room, the air thick with incense and something both unknown and eerily familiar, and with Whole Foods and Chipotle across the street yet light years away, it felt just right.

Unless she told you something you didn't want to hear.

"The book you are publishing. It is too soon," she said unemotionally one day. "There is a big thing missing in it—a major part, a significant experience ... it's not the right time," she said matter-of-factly.

A wave of dread washed over me as I thought about having uploaded the last and final manuscript of *Jumping the Picket Fence* to CreateSpace, Amazon's self-publishing platform, that very morning. I had been giddy in the moment, during that one click when all of the major details of my life so far, the events that had led us down an unconventional path, were beamed up into the stratosphere. All I had yet to do was approve the printed sample copy that was to come in the mail, and the fourteen years of grueling energy it had taken to document the journey would be over.

It had seemed only natural to write the book—our family had chosen to live a different life, most of which we had spent abroad or traveling. The story began when our marriage was at a near breaking point. I felt like I had lost my center, my true north. I had a burning desire to do anything but settle into a comfortable life with our small business and two young children. I didn't know what I was looking for or where to find it, but I knew a big world was out there, and I was desperate to be useful within it. After logical resistance and a few heated arguments, my husband, John, surrendered.

We left the US and settled in the south of France with our first two children, Nick and Emma. We renovated a farmhouse and later started a villa rental business. Six years later, our family expanded as our third child, Isabelle, was brought into our fold from China. I found my place, albeit in a roundabout way, in the humanitarian world I had always dreamed of being a part of. I built a philanthropic travel company and later co-founded a foundation that helped grassroots programs in marginalized areas seek their fair access to education, health services, and basic human rights. The years had been adventurous and exciting, at times risky and unsettling, but mostly they had restored our faith that something significant was out there. Whatever it was, it was bigger than us—and it mattered.

I had made a vow to myself in writing the book. I wanted to be honest, to share the whole story and not just what appeared to be a pretty ending. I had felt terribly lost and lonely at times in my journey—in myself, in my motherhood, and in trying to find a useful place for a genuine desire to contribute to a world that had so much wrong with it. And while we had set out into the intimidating philanthropic arena with beautiful intentions and hopes of making a difference, we had been naive and underexperienced. I was sure there could be value in sharing the mistakes I had made and the lessons we had learned along the way. I had sat in front of brave individuals who had faced horrible atrocities, yet had found a strength and power in themselves to walk through them to find a better place on the other side. My greatest lessons had been taught by their willingness to share their vulnerability, and I challenged myself to do the same.

With our family now settled in Los Angeles, the foundation soundly on its feet, and *Jumping the Picket Fence* ready to be released, I yearned for normalcy after so many years of rugged travel and nonprofit-building. I was happily ending a huge period in my life and was more than ready to finally tick the box and say—this upload is ready; this is complete.

"Well it's already in the queue for publishing," I said to Tauheedah. "GoPhilanthropic has its annual fundraising event at the beginning of January here in LA, and the book launch has been timed with the event. I mean, I suppose I could put the brakes on, but things are in motion. I feel it is a little too late to stop. Do you think I am making a major mistake by following through?"

Tauheedah looked off into the distance, her eyes dancing up and down, her head turning gently as if she was scanning and listening to something or someone at the same time.

"Not really," she finally said. "You can carry on," she continued, shaking her head from side to side, her thin black braids moving in concert.

"But there is something missing. I am sure of it."

1

NIGHTMARES IN KATHMANDU

*Out beyond ideas of wrongdoing and rightdoing
there is a field. I'll meet you there.*

—Rumi

APRIL 25, 2015—THREE MONTHS LATER

I pulled out the oversized key and unlocked the ancient padlock that secured the wooden door of my hotel room. The porter placed my suitcase gently on a leather case holder near the entrance, then turned to leave.

"Namaste," I said, bowing slightly, palms together.

I quickly walked over to the antique desk. Pulling my computer, cell phone, and notepad from my bag, I placed them on the desk and settled into the chair. The sun had not managed to peek through the clouds that day, and the room felt dark and cold. A chill ran up my back and down the length of my bare arms. I wandered over to my suitcase, opened it up, and grabbed my woolen sweater that was lying on top of a heap of dirty clothes. It was high time to do some wash, but I was due to fly back to Delhi the next day, then onward home to Los Angeles. A case full of foreign-smelling clothes was always a sign of a good voyage. You never have a way of knowing, as you pack your things, crisply folded and tidy before leaving, what you will encounter in your time away, how it will change the way you see things.

As I pulled on my sweater, I glanced at the bathroom door—my mind wandering to the thought of a long-needed soak in the bath. Peeking further around the corner, I saw a deep, white porcelain tub lined with small square handmade local soaps and plush white towels. *God, that is tempting.* The visits to grassroots nonprofit organizations (NGOs) during the past week, coupled with two days of trekking with Raj, a Nepali friend who owns the Social Tours travel agency that supported social development in Nepal through tourism, were enough to have me stripping off the sweater, along with the rest of my clothes, and running the warm water.

As I stood naked, the tub halfway full, I got an odd feeling, a sudden urge to turn off the water and put my clothes back on. *I had better get to my notes*, I told myself. There's no time to indulge in a bath.

I returned to the task of transcribing my notes, my stomach reminding me that I had skipped breakfast and had forgone grabbing lunch as I marched past the café downstairs and up the flight of stairs to my room after checking in. My schedule was too tight for lunch, as I was due to meet with the director of Little Sisters, a program offering school sponsorship to economically disadvantaged Nepali girls. I was also anxious to capture my impressions from this morning's meeting with an inspiring young change-agent, Indra Prasad, who had built a school for children who lacked access to education outside of Bhaktapur. We had spent hours together discussing his belief that parents, no matter how economically challenged, should be expected to invest in their children's future. "It can't be a handout," he had said emphatically.

Indra's words played over in my mind during the bumpy drive to the hotel back in Kathmandu. We were hearing this more and more from the grassroots partners we had formed relationships with at the foundation. Efforts to create better futures for people in need had to begin with their involvement. They were the key players in their own transformation. Somehow something so basic could be easily overlooked or minimized by the various stakeholders who were engaged in fixing what seemed broken. Just get the money where it needs to go, where it can have the most impact, was oftentimes a donor's mantra.

Out of the blue, I felt a shaking beneath my feet. I stopped typing on my laptop and turned my full attention to the sound of a deep rumble. I tried to place the noise—maybe a generator, commonly used here in Kathmandu as they suffer from frequent power outages. At one point, I had asked around about why power outages happened so often, but had never gotten a straight answer. A few said that the lack of power was one of the many residual effects of Nepal's decade-long civil war. Poor infrastructure, political instability, and corruption still plagued the country. *Most hotels seemed to kick their generators into gear late afternoon,* I thought to myself. I glanced at the time on my phone—11:55 a.m.— it was a bit early for that.

The shaking became more intense, the rumbling more power-ful. Turning around to look out the window, I noticed the two water bottles on the coffee table suddenly topple over. A sickening feeling washed over me, and without thinking, I stood up, only to be pushed to the side by a violent tremor. My eyes moved in a circle from the table to the walls to the ceiling, then back to the table, until I realized that they were strangely no longer solid and flat. They were moving, like waves on an ocean, soft and fluid. Or were they melting?

This is not good. I'm either hallucinating or something terribly wrong is happening. My instinct was to run, but I couldn't move my body. It was paralyzed, like in those dreams where you are willing your legs into motion, and they just don't budge. But this felt all too real to be a dream.

I waited for the unsettling motion to stop, but it persisted, intensifying with every second. The sound of shaking buildings continued but was now combined with a new noise—moving furniture, which had become solid again, screaming around the floor. I watched as the tall cabinet slid across the room. But the worst was about to come—the deafening sound of an entire building collapsing echoed across the valley, followed by piercing screams coming from both near and far.

A bomb. There's been a bombing. I was sure of it now. Glass shattered from the courtyard below; the cry of terrified voices shook my body and mind out of its fear-induced inactivity. I glanced at the door to my room, now swinging wildly, opening then closing, the big keys banging loudly as they smacked against a door that no longer fit into its frame. Big, bright, warm light streamed from the opening, and I suddenly knew my job, my way out, was to follow it. Now.

But for a brief millisecond before heading out the door, I looked back through the window of my room, out toward the gray, cold sky. Different objects, I couldn't make out what they were, flew through the air. The objects were then replaced, as if on a screen of consciousness, by the faces of my family. One by one their images lingered—my husband, John, the love of my life. Nick, almost a grown man of eighteen. Emma, sixteen, and dear Isabelle, only nine. She can't lose another mother. Then a sickening feeling flushed through my body. I couldn't place it at first. It wasn't fear, anger, or sadness. It was an emotion I hadn't quite fully experienced in a long, long time, maybe since childhood when all feelings seem purer and more heightened. Dread. Yes, that's what it was. Dread enveloped me, spreading all over me, as I realized that this might be it, the end. My time had come. Waves of grief then coursed through my veins. *No, not yet, it can't be yet. It went by too quickly. There are things I still need to do.*

The bedroom door smacked loudly again, and at that moment, only one thought raced through my mind—*GET OUT*. I scrambled across the floor as it moved violently, throwing me into the side of the bed, then over to the other side of the room to the TV stand. I finally made my way out of the door to the top of the stairs, and with no time for steps, I lunged down the flights of stairs, my hands out by my sides as I was tossed from one wall to another. I landed in a heap on the stone terrace outside the ancient building.

For a brief second I felt relief—I had made it out alive. *OK, I'm OK.* I breathed deeply and looked down at my feet and realized I had lost a sandal. *But I am safe, from this bomb or whatever this is. It must be over.*

Just then, a tall man approached me, all color drained from his face. "Earthquake," he said firmly. I guess it should have been clearer to me earlier, but I had never lived through one before, apart from a few light tremors felt during our trips to Costa Rica. I had never felt such violence from the earth, had never known this destructive side of her.

I stumbled to my feet, brushed off my jeans, and lifted my head to take in the scene. I noticed the little lunch café that I had considered eating at earlier had collapsed on one side and was reduced to a pile of stones and glass. Staff in their uniforms, and guests in both business clothes and bathing suits, were running from every doorway and stairwell, all headed toward the pool area, where they were gathering in a disorderly crowd. Everyone looked stunned and stone-figured, locked in an internal world of panic. People used their hands to cover their faces and their ears, blocking out the deafening sounds of disaster around us.

It was then that I looked up and noticed a three-foot wall of water coming out of the pool and onto the patio where we were all huddled. The crowd scrambled and fled in every which direction. The torrent of water swept forcefully underneath my feet, taking away my other sandal as it surged to the other side of the terrace. Rock tiles, now split and broken, pushed up out of the ground, and a massive clay planter tumbled from the ledge next to me. Cracking, crumbling, screaming—*When will this be over? Make it stop.*

I slipped into full panic mode and ran up to the closest person to me—a man, he looked German, or maybe Danish. I grabbed the side of his arm and started shaking him. "What do we do— where do we go?" I yelled. He was frozen and unresponsive, his eyes glassed over; he pulled his arm away from me. Frustrated, I turned my attention to the woman at his side, and looking desperately at her, I repeated, "What do we do?" She just gazed at me, through me, vacant and lost. I held her elbows, my face and body so close to hers that for a moment, I noticed tiny white bumps on her face. She remained silent, but then gripped me tighter as a violent aftershock shook the courtyard, forcing everyone closer to each other. We all stared up to the sky and to the ancient hotel building walls surrounding us, wondering when they would come tumbling down.

Dwarika's wasn't just any hotel—it was a monument in time, steeped in decades of Nepali history and culture. When I had heard it was an experience in itself, like staying in a museum, I knew it was a place I had to visit. A few days earlier, I had enjoyed reading about the origins, how Dwarika Das Shrestha, a young man with a passion for old wood carvings and Newari heritage, had created a bold vision for a hotel that challenged the drive to make the city more modern. The story went that the young man was jogging past the ruins of an old building in front of the ancient palatial complex of Kathmandu's Newar kings when he confronted two carpenters sawing off the intricate carvings on an old wooden pillar and using them to keep their fire going. Shocked that such beautiful historical artifacts could be reduced to kindling, he bought the ancient pieces of wood, later collecting similar masterpieces from all around the city. These simple actions formed the beginnings of what would be a lifetime built around conserving, honoring, and sharing Nepal's rich and beautiful history.

Being at Dwarika's felt like you were taking a step back in time—the floors creaked, and the air smelled like a mixture of incense and wood. On that morning when I had arrived, it was filled with a blend of tourists, businesspeople, and teams of trekkers making their way to Everest basecamp at the height of the season. A buzz was in the air as porters moved piles of gear into vans. The staff at the reception area were swiftly efficient, attentive, and warm, not knowing the day would take such a tragic turn.

I released my grip on the woman I was clutching, as a smartly dressed staff member suddenly took command, directing us all to the back of the hotel where the courtyard extended away from the older parts of the building. "Please everyone, move quickly—come this way." Following him, we huddled near two small trees, as if they could protect us from anything. I noticed several hotel staff carefully directing an older Nepali woman and her dogs to a wooden bench near the trees. I learned later that she was Mrs. Dwarika herself—wife of the former Dwarika Das Shrestha, who had died some years earlier. The dog, also old and fragile, remained glued to the side of her leg, yet crouched on the ground, as if listening closely to the earth's inner turmoil while we all rushed about on its surface.

There were maybe forty of us at that point, everyone hanging on to somebody as one aftershock blended into another. A man with a clipboard began to make the rounds, attempting to get a head count of the guests who were registered and still on the premises. With it being midday, many guests had been out and about visiting the main temples—Swayambhunath, Pashupatinath, Boudhanath, or the famous Durbar Square that faced the old Royal Palace, a marvel of centuries-old architecture. Seven UNESCO World Heritage sites were in the valley. That morning, I had taken a private walking tour in the ancient city of Bhaktapur, referred to as the "place of devotees," only eight miles or so from the center of Kathmandu. Even at five in the morning, the dusty, narrow cobblestone streets had been a sea of soft and gentle movement, of quiet daily ritual. I'd heard a light patter of feet shuffling and the faint tinkling of bells as people, young and old, made their rounds around the small city temples, lighting candles and incense, circling the prayer wheels, then washing discreetly at various water pumps.

I had stopped several times on my walk to take in the distinct beauty of the moment, the soft murmur of prayers, the silent meditations. *What a serene and peaceful way to begin a day*, I had thought to myself as small flocks of birds swooped in and out of the ancient courtyards. Our culture in the West didn't seem to greet each morning with such gentleness. I sat for some time on a small broken temple step and waited for the sun to slowly rise, but it never did appear from behind the gray clouds that morning.

As we were being relocated to the back terrace, I left the German couple and migrated toward an American couple—I was seeking safety, and they looked kind and caring. After making eye contact, I slid naturally into an embrace with the woman, and cried instantly. It was strange, almost instinctual, to be so intimate with someone you had never met before. In a matter of minutes, it felt like we had known each other for years. In between bouts of my crying, we managed to exchange names and ask each other what we were doing in Kathmandu.

"My name is Lydia, and I have three children. I'm here doing NGO work."

"My name is Rowena. This is my husband, Joe. We live in Boston, and have two girls in their early twenties."

Rowena and I spent the next half hour filling each other in on our lives. Tucked into her arms and listening to her talk reminded me of my Mum, how her voice could soothe any bad situation— how after a few moments of sobbing, everything would always feel OK.

"So how did you get into NGO work? Tell me about that," she asked. Part of me knew that she was simply getting me to talk to get my mind off of the situation. It was a loving mother tactic I had used myself with my own children.

"Well the whole thing began after we left the US and moved to France. We traveled a lot during this time, with our two children, to all of the places we had always dreamed of going. We were incredibly fortunate to be able to discover the world, but the more we stretched out, the more we realized we had been living in a comfortable, naïve, privileged bubble," I began. "We visited places that experienced huge numbers of tourists each year, yet where communities still struggled with the very basics, like clean water and access to health services and education. In Cambodia, the newly built hotels and tourist establishments were surrounded by people living in extreme poverty. We started to get off the main road to see what existed beyond what the tourists were being dished up. What we found was amazing—we met incredible people and programs rebuilding from years of devastating genocide, yet tourists, like us, would come and go without knowing they existed. They would leave not only unaware of the issues these communities faced, but they had missed out on understanding how people were bravely forging a way forward."

It had seemed unbelievable to me; it felt wrong and selfish to come and take in the magnificence of a place but to leave without seeing the full picture. I felt that ignorance often blinded us, not a lack of care. And on the part of the important programs and local efforts, it was a lack of being heard and noticed that was the problem. They needed connection to the global community, a way to voice and share what they were doing—they needed to be seen.

Another aftershock rolled through the valley before I could explain that the next ten years of building a philanthropic travel company and a foundation based on these early ideas would reveal a much more complicated task at hand. Thousands of moving, complex pieces in the "giving world" had to be considered, and the net result was not always positive. Funding could harm and helping when you didn't fully understand could, in fact, be destructive. Unbeknownst to me at the time, it would require experience I didn't have yet.

When the trembling finally tapered, people loosened their grips and began to separate, giving each other small berths to resume some sense of stability. Some walked in circles; others sat on the ground with their heads in their hands. Scanning the courtyard, I noticed that the looks on the faces of the Nepalese had a different magnitude of panic and concern. Tragedy does not hit us all equally. They, unlike me, had children, wives, husbands, mothers, and fathers here in Nepal to worry about. Were they alive? Were they safe? Mine were asleep, safe and protected in California. They had families, homes, businesses, and livelihoods to consider. I noticed people making futile attempts on their phones to make calls out, but it was clear there was no cell service. Looking down at my bare feet, I wondered what was happening outside of Dwarika's walls, and what was going to happen next.

A tall and classy foreign woman veered over to Rowena and Joe and me. I had already noticed her from across the courtyard. She seemed to be alone, and I had admired how strong she appeared, maybe even a little stoic—she wasn't clinging to or hugging anyone like the rest of us. She made her way over to us, and we shared introductions. "Hi, I am Dominique. I live in Australia but am originally French Canadian," she said in a uniquely blended accent. I shared that I, too, was Canadian, from Ottawa.

"I had always dreamed of hiking Everest, but as I have gotten older, I've shifted my goal to simply getting to base camp. I was scheduled to trek last year, but it had been cancelled due to an ice avalanche that killed sixteen climbing Sherpas in the Khumbu Icefall. This is my second attempt, and I have to admit that my friends and family thought I was testing fate to come again. I was supposed to have been at base camp already, but there was an issue with my passport. I've been waiting it out at Dwarika's," she continued.

Feeling immediately comfortable with each other, we found a place to sit down on the ground and kept our conversations going. We chatted about what possessions we each had on us. Rowena had a purse; Dominique had her phone and room key. "There's a story behind this, though," she said chuckling. "I had had a past experience where my room was robbed in a hotel, so even as the earthquake began, I made my way back across the room to get my key so that I could lock the door behind me. It's incredible, isn't it, what you do in the moment of things—how silly it was that I needed to lock the door," she said as she looked at the key in her hand.

"I have my own key story," chimed in Ro. "We arrived at Dwarika's this morning, feeling unusually spiritual after spending a week in Bhutan. Our guide arrived to take us to tour Durbar Square. Fortunately, he sensed we were tired and suggested that we postpone the tour and rest at the hotel."

She continued, "The hotel room door had a padlock, which could only be locked and unlocked from outside of the room. Joe locked the door from the outside so that I could rest undisturbed, then headed to the pool area to use the Wi-Fi. I heard music coming from across the road—it sort of called to me, so I abandoned the idea of the nap, dialed up the front desk to release me from the room, and headed to the festival where the music had been coming from. On my way back to the room, I saw Joe, and we decided to have lunch. We stopped in the hotel courtyard, perused the lunch menu items on display and moved on. We parked ourselves at a table next to a heavy, old wooden structure where a huge iron bell was hanging. For some reason, I wasn't comfortable there, so we got up and walked to a different table. As soon as we sat, a huge flock of birds flew noisily overhead, dogs barked, and monkeys screeched. Then the earth rumbled and shook—the noise was deafening. Joe wondered what was happening, and since I had been in an earthquake previously, albeit a much smaller one, I knew. I told him, "This is an earthquake. A big one." Just then, the table near where Joe had been sitting just minutes before at the pool crashed into plate glass windows, shattering them, and the massive iron bell crashed to the ground."

It was clear that in telling us the story, Ro was only beginning to process what had just happened to her. You could tell she hadn't quite come to terms with how a few seemingly unimportant decisions had saved them from serious harm.

I began to consider that all my essentials—phone, passport, purse, and laptop—were in my hotel room. I again glanced down at my bare feet. Shoes would probably be a good thing right now. Just at that moment, someone from the hotel approached me and said, "Here, take these—there is glass everywhere," then forced the slippers into my hands. I looked at them—they were big and floppy, and I set them down beside me. It seemed silly, but I wanted my feet to feel the earth—to be able to read her, to know when the rumbling would begin again.

I heard the soft sounds of crying over my left shoulder. Turning toward the two trees, I noticed a Nepalese woman sitting on a bench, shaking uncontrollably. A younger male staff member was crouched at her feet, trying to soothe her. She was holding her phone and sobbing as she stared blankly at it. She couldn't have been much older than my daughter Emma, eighteen, maybe nineteen, no more. I approached her and looked at her face, wrought with fear and anguish. "Are you OK?" I asked, not knowing if she spoke English. I placed my hand on her back and rubbed it, an act that under any other circumstance might not have been culturally appropriate, yet was instinctual for me in the moment. The male staff member ran off to fetch some water for her to sip. She looked at me and placed her hands in prayer position in front of her heart. "I'm sorry," she kept saying over and over. "I'm so sorry. It is my mother." She continued in quiet, deliberate words. "I am so scared for my mother. She is alone at home. I don't know if she is OK."

I didn't know what to tell her, what to say. The pain and grief of not knowing if someone you love is safe must have been all-consuming, and I had no way to comfort her other than sitting next to her. I felt useless.

Birds suddenly began to squawk, flying frantically in circles. The dog sitting next to Madame Dwarika picked his head up and let out a long and agonizing moan; it was a sound I had never heard before and one I have yet to hear again. Seconds later, another massive aftershock came through like a wave across the ocean. We would later learn that it reached 6.6 magnitude, nearly as big as the earthquake itself. Everyone stopped what they were doing, and a terrible, cold silence set in before the earth gave in once more to a deep, fathomless, bottomless violence. Everyone succumbed to the same reaction—we looked up to the sky and made silent prayers.

2

MOMMA EARTH AND POPPA SKY

*If you don't rise to the occasion, the best of you will die
and the rest will not amount to anything.*

—Lily Yeh

BETWEEN TREMORS, the birds began to chirp again, as if telling all of us it was OK to breathe—for a while. After several hours of pacing, sharing details of our lives, and gasping during the aftershocks, we began to make ourselves more comfortable, staking out territory on the wooden benches or chairs. Rowena, Joe, Dominique, and I found mats from the sun loungers and tried to place them comfortably on the ground.

"Oh my—it's Inez," yelled Dominique as she popped up to greet a tall, middle-aged European woman who had sauntered into the back courtyard, her long blond hair loosely twisted on one shoulder. Her forehead was smeared with vibrant colors, and she looked in great form—not shaken at all.

Dominique had befriended Inez in the days before and had been terribly worried when she hadn't returned from the festival she left for that morning, the same one Rowena had visited at the Hindu temple across the street. It was clear Inez was somewhat unaware of the extent of what had happened. *Maybe she has smoked something, or maybe,* I started to wish hopefully, since she had come in from the outside, *it's not all bad out there beyond these walls after all.*

Dominique made the introductions while Inez looked around disapprovingly at our rather messy makeshift camp, at people settling in for the night.

"What's happening out there?" I asked impatiently. "How bad is it?"

"I was under this tent when it happened, and there was a lot of music and it was a bit chaotic anyway, so it was really hard to tell—it doesn't seem so bad. Why?" she asked a little nonchalantly.

"I think it is worse than you think, Inez. We aren't allowed in any of the buildings," said Dominique. "It's too dangerous."

"Hmmm. Shit. Well, I'm worried my singing bowl is going to be dented—I left it on the bed," Inez said disappointedly. "It won't sing like it is supposed to. And my new tattoo, I need to clean it," she continued. I sat on my mat, amazed at her reaction. Maybe this was her way of coping, of convincing herself that none of it was real, and it wasn't life-threatening.

"I am just going to go to my room. I can't sleep here. No one can tell me I can't go," she said firmly in her Swiss accent.

Dominique looked at me with doubtful eyes, then over to Inez.

"I think we are staying here tonight," said Dominique. "Come here, stop fussing with the tattoo. Let me look at it," she said tenderly, flinging Inez's long hair over her shoulder to inspect her neck. "It looks just fine. Come and settle down, there's room here on the mat," she said, patting the space next to her.

At around 5 p.m., we were told that we might be able to enter our rooms briefly to get out some warm clothes and other essentials. The energy of the crowd immediately lifted, but minutes after the announcement, the earth trembled and snubbed any plan for going anywhere. The sun began to set, and we accepted the reality of sleeping under the stars, actually a rather comforting thought. I didn't want to go anywhere near the buildings. A strange, quiet eeriness filled the air as the light slipped away, a dampness spreading itself across the courtyard and into our bodies.

Out of the blue, we were startled by a middle-aged European man who began to shout—I couldn't quite make out what he said but it was loud and rather obnoxious; he was most certainly barking at someone. I turned my attention and saw he was directing his orders at a young man wearing a hotel uniform. "There must be beer in this place," he yelled, his face turning bright red. "Can you please find us some beer," he repeated, louder this time.

The courtyard went silent, everyone glared at him and the group of men sitting with him. Minutes later, his friends shifted uncomfortably in their seats as they were brought their drinks, miraculously appearing from somewhere. I worried that the staff member must have fetched the beers from inside the hotel unless there was a stash somewhere in an outside bar. Knowing how unsafe it was to enter the hotel, I hoped the latter was the case. Either way, it was such an ugly display, and I was deeply embarrassed at his behavior. *There's always an asshole*, I thought to myself, but in this situation, it felt magnified beyond comprehension. In the moment, he represented a privileged Westerner, one who was an additional burden during a disastrous moment, yet who was also hell-bent on maintaining his sense of entitlement.

It captured all that was wrong with so much of what I was exposed to daily; the inequities that existed here in Nepal, at home in the US, in France where I lived, and all over the world—a misuse of power and influence that has been simply accepted for far too long. But I couldn't deny that I, too, was part of the machine that drove these harmful dynamics. I had built a life around trying to make things right, but it didn't change the painful reality that I had been offered gifts while others, so many others, were being denied.

The hotel staff started making the rounds, first passing plates of oatmeal cookies followed by water bottles. I noticed several guests stockpiling their water, then returning for more. An hour later, folding tables with tablecloths were set up, from which the staff cooked hot steaming pots of soup and noodles. A young server approached my mat gingerly, with respect, as if entering my private room. "I am sorry for the simplicity of the meal, ma'am," he said as he leaned over to offer me a bowl of soup. I was baffled—shocked and uncomfortable to be served anything. *We should all muck in*, I thought. *Show us how. Show us where. Please. We are all in this together. This is your country. You don't need to serve me.* How quickly roles had been resumed.

"No thank you. Namaste, namaste," I said. "That is so very kind of you. I am not so hungry," was all I mustered in my confusion.

I considered the past hours and how, at the outset, in a matter of a few violent minutes, who we were, our names and titles, and what we had accomplished in life ceased to matter. We were all together, a mess of people, all shapes and sizes, from here and from there, some scared, some strong, grabbing onto one another for dear life. In such a short time, we had shared, cried, and prayed together. Whether we were working in the hotel or staying in the hotel held no value as the buildings came down around us, one after the other. But as I was offered this simple bowl of noodle soup, put together under such extreme conditions, I just couldn't accept such a quick return to this division of roles, this separation. I couldn't fathom being cared for as a guest. I didn't want to eat soup in the moment like that, in that way. "What could I offer?" seemed a better question at the time—one that had haunted me, and would continue to, for a long time.

I watched as two staff members suddenly approached a man, his uniform and apron looking like he worked in the kitchen. He was told something that afterward had him buckling to his knees, crying out loud, cupping his face. He was quickly escorted out of the front archway, outside, and into whatever madness existed out there. Whispers circulated from one group to the next until it reached us—"It's his wife," someone said. "It's not good news."

Until this point, there had been no way to know the extent of the disaster. All we had to go on were the initial, horrifying sounds of what were clearly buildings coming down. One could only imagine lives had been lost, most likely many. But as we were settling in for the evening, news finally started coming in.

"The roof of the airport has come down," someone said. "It's closed and there is no chance to get out."

"Hundreds of people have died in Dharahara Tower in Durbar Square," someone else stated. Dharahara Tower was a beautiful structure, built in the 1800s, with a spiral staircase with 213 steps. It was a popular spot to take in the sweeping views of the Kathmandu Valley from its eighth floor circular balcony.

"Durbar Square is basically no longer," someone else added.

Bhaktapur, where I had witnessed the magic and beauty of daily sacred rituals that morning, was said to be reduced to rubble. Then a group sitting next to us leaned over and shared their latest information. "Everest base camp has been hit hard with an avalanche—teams have been wiped out." I turned to Dominique, her eyes instantly welled with tears. "Oh dear God," she whispered under her breath.

It was impossible to know what was real and what wasn't. The information seemed to be coming through only one or two sources, the few people who were able to communicate on their cell phones and from the men in uniforms who gathered outside the courtyard near Dwarika's front doors. We were not allowed to leave the premises, and nobody else appeared to have any cell reception. I saw a woman whom I deduced to be the owner of the hotel, probably the daughter of the founding father. She had an incredibly commanding presence, powerful yet graceful, and an unmistakable resemblance to the older woman with the dog. She was now constantly on her phone, nodding, making notes, gathering information. We found out later that only some of the news that we had heard had been true—and the worst of it was only to emerge in the following days.

Night came and along with it, a blanket of cold, heavy air. Lying down on my mat next to the two little trees that had become my shelter, I found solace in facing rows of traditional Buddhist prayer wheels, maybe eight or so, five or six feet high. I stared at their elegant shape, their cylindrical form, made from a combination of metal and wood. I pictured the feel of them on my fingertips, spinning freely one after the other. The wheels, inscribed with mantras on both the outsides and insides, are supposed to represent the physical manifestation of "turning the wheel of Dharma," which is believed to be the cosmic law and order in the teachings of Buddha. In spinning the wheel, one hopes to release all that is negative within us and to gain the wisdom sought in enlightenment.

I moved my focus from the wheel up to the dark night sky where, since the beginning of time, we have looked for hope and answers. That great, endless expansiveness has held our dreams, our beliefs in possibilities. My gaze then moved to the soft, red earth underneath me, a place that extends beyond what we could measure—to some great, warm source where the birth of everything takes place. *Poppa Sky and Momma Earth*, I thought to myself, *with us and our prayer wheels in between.*

It was as if all of humanity was caught between the spirit world above and the great governing maternal source below, and our task was to listen, to decipher the language between them. There are answers in there. *What are you saying? What are we here to learn? What are we being called to do?*

I curled up, placing a towel over my head, trying to capture the warmth of my own breath, and maybe, if I was lucky, a way to escape through sleep. But as I shut my eyes, visions of my time in Nepal, of the people I had met, flashed across the screen in my mind. I saw Shyam Pokharel and the team at SASANE, brave survivors of human trafficking. I hadn't anticipated experiencing such a well of strength when I had walked through the iron gate that protected their simple offices on the outskirts of the city. The realities of human trafficking suddenly became very real to me as they explained their work, which offered paralegal training to female survivors. After passing their exams, the women were then assigned to police stations around Nepal, where they extended legal services, free of charge, to other survivors of trafficking and gender-based violence. The program not only helped survivors reintegrate into society with dignity, but it provided the opportunity for them to reclaim their sense of rights and dignity and to encourage others to do the same.

After a dusty forty-five minute drive outside of the city, I had met Rita Thapa, founder of TEWA. Rita was a trailblazer, a force of nature, who believed in the possibilities of a sustainable development model in what had become an overly aid-dependent Nepal. TEWA aimed to increase the self-reliance of Nepalis by reducing dependency on foreign donors. By mobilizing hundreds of volunteers, TEWA raised money from Nepali citizens, those who had the economic ability to do so easily, but also those who didn't—a radical concept for a country considered so economically challenged. In doing so, Rita felt there was both power and healing in involving everyday citizens, who she believed wanted to do their part in rebuilding their own country from the grassroots upward. Funding from TEWA allowed the organization to then make small grants to local women's associations.

I had visited the village of Dadaguan, where a small community of subsistence farmers were earning their livelihoods from making and selling local grain alcohol. Dhorje, the village's passionate school principal, believed in the potential of the village's youth and was devoted to empowering the government teachers who received pitiful government salaries. Despite the lack of investment in this most essential human capital, he had cobbled together his dream of offering teachers the training and support they needed to be great educators, believing that children could thrive, no matter what their economic situation, if they were encouraged to learn. The school was running on financial fumes with the little they received from the local municipality and from a few foreign donors.

These rich and insightful exchanges had all taken place in the past days, yet it seemed an eternity had passed. But the memory that stuck with me the most was one that was much less hopeful, and it would haunt me for years to come. I had visited a small shelter for girls only the day before. Raj and I had just finished our trekking in the town where I was due to visit the shelter. It made logistical sense, even though we were sweaty and exhausted from hours of hiking, to stop by before dropping me off at my hotel in Bhaktapur. I had been referred to the girls' home by Carol, a young college student from the US who had asked her guide to take her and her classmates to visit an orphanage as a part of their recent tour in Nepal. After spending heartwarming time with the girls, the group decided to raise funds for them upon returning home. Carol called me to see if GoPhilanthropic could transfer some money. After listening to her story, I gently explained to her why her request was not a simple one—why it, in fact, was a dangerous one that could perpetuate a corrupt system that led to the trafficking of children into fake orphanages.

Visiting, donating, or volunteering at an orphanage in developing countries has become more and more popular over the past decades; it has become a cherished line item on a resume—global altruism at work. I explained to Carol that more than eight million children live in residential care institutions globally, despite the fact that around 80 percent of these children have parents, and even more have extended family who could care for them. Unfortunately, the institutionalization of children, in many cases, has been driven by the well-meaning but uninformed support of foreign donors, orphanage voluntourism, and the supply chain of people, money, and resources that drive the orphanage industry. In Nepal, vulnerable children who live in rural areas lacking education are lured away from their parents by traffickers who make money on both ends—from desperate parents who want a better life for their children and from foreign volunteers who are completely unaware of the implications of their funding. Children are forced to lie about their backgrounds in order to convince tourists and volunteers that they are "orphans," so the traffickers can profit from people's generosity. As a consequence, many orphanages have become a lucrative, corrupt, and abusive business funded by well-intentioned donors.

"Carol, you can see the pattern. It's only logical that with all the charity flowing into these institutions, corruption has played a significant part in the thousands of orphanages that have popped up like weeds over the past couple of decades. In many countries, owning and running an orphanage has now become an incredibly profitable business, with foreign donations serving as income. There is a decent chance that the girls in that home are not orphans at all, and they have been used as pawns in a vicious scheme. There is a much safer and more effective way to support vulnerable children, and it needs to involve trusted and dedicated organizations who know the landscape."

I knew that Carol was disappointed, but her experience was far too common, and GoPhil was deeply committed to advocating against funding orphanages whenever it could. Our years of experience working in underserved communities had taught us firsthand lessons in how foreign support to institutions, small or large, could play a role in separating children from their families. As a result, GoPhil had made a decision to focus our funding toward building healthier families and stronger communities so that children would be less likely to end up in an institution.

"Look—I'm headed to Nepal in a few weeks," I told Carol. "Pass me the contact information for the shelter, and I will check it out. I'll let you know what I find when I get back." Carol shared in a follow-up email that her main contact to the shelter was through her guide, a telltale sign that something was amiss. Having her communicate through him exclusively, he could ensure his cut of the donations that came through.

The moment I entered the home, every hair on the back of my neck stood on end. While far from being an expert, I had been to dozens of shelters and orphanages over the years and had gathered enough experience to recognize key indicators of child exploitation. Properly run institutions had strict policies in place protecting the children from visitors being paraded through their homes day and night, snapping pictures as if they were in a zoo. Then there were a variety of variables to look for—their local registrations, the qualifications of their staff, whether they were professionally trained, and staff-to-child ratio. How the children appeared was also a sign; typically the dirtier they were, the more they would be able to solicit easy donations.

As we walked through the front gate, the girls, all between the ages of about seven and twelve, were lined up to greet us one by one with flowers and what felt like rehearsed, shy smiles. While their hair was combed back neatly, they were clearly very unclean, and their clothes, visibly dirty, hung off their little frail bodies. A tall, foreboding man stood at the main door, introducing himself as the director. He ushered us into the cold, two-story concrete building, into an empty office room.

Instinctively, I looked over my shoulder to make sure Raj was behind me; normally I am alone on these visits, but was glad to have him at my side. We sat down, and I pulled out my notebook to run through some initial introductory questions, reviewing the basics of the shelter, its history, funding partners, and the daily schedule for the girls. In reality, only professionals can do a thorough and proper assessment. They do this by looking at written records, talking with the children and the staff, and by assessing the material conditions in the orphanage. It was a difficult and skilled job and needed to be conducted by people who spoke Nepali and really understood the context. Even then, it was still a tough judgment at times because so much deceit was involved.

The director had little to say to me, besides the fact that they had only one donor, a group of Japanese tourists who had visited some years before. It had been some time since they had sent any money, and things were getting desperate. He went on to explain that he also worked at a hotel close by—and that he tried to bring other tourists in to see the girls in hopes that they would donate.

I could feel my heart begin to race while a sick and eerie feeling rushed over me. A terrible, sinking suspicion formed in my mind that the girls had been trafficked, that they were in a place they couldn't escape from. After about thirty minutes into our discussion, I felt an immediate impulse to leave.

Knowing the dangers of the situation at hand, and that I couldn't, nor shouldn't, do anything myself, I gathered as much data as I could without letting on to the director that I had my suspicions. Data and information about the risks of orphanage tourism were only just emerging at the time; even a year later, we never would have visited the shelter ourselves, instead passing on the details to knowledgeable local NGOs who work carefully with authorities to investigate each shelter. Luckily, I did something that we typically don't do out of respect for privacy and protection for the people and organizations we visit. I took a quick photo of the girls and myself with my phone before leaving, knowing that it could be one of the only means of identifying the girls later.

We climbed back into the car, where Raj and I just looked at each other in disbelief.

"Whatever is happening in there is not right," I said.

"No it's not, Lydia—no it is not."

After checking into the Hotel Heritage, I dropped my bags and sunk into the wooden chair next to the bed as the sunlight faded across the ancient city of Bhaktapur. I was numb. I couldn't believe what I had just experienced. We had been working with shelters for years, and I had seen children in many desperate situations—living in terribly underserved areas in rural Cambodia, in New Delhi where their mothers were trapped in bonded sex labor and in the heart of Kibera slums in Nairobi, where 90 percent of children with HIV went without treatment. What made this so different was unclear to me in that moment. Perhaps it had been the vacant look in their eyes—and not just from one of them but from each one of them. It was a look that said, "Are you going to be just like the rest who come and go with your notebook and your questions and your incessant need to feel as though you are doing something important in the world, yet at the end of the day you get into your white van and go back to your hotel, and to your home far away where we will become a distant thought."

It was as if something within me until that point had buffered me, had protected me from the real truth that evil existed—that this world was truly and certainly a terribly unjust, inhumane place for some, and not for others. What I had seen in their eyes was a lack of hope that the future held anything for them. They had accepted that as their fate.

Fumbling through my bag in search of the candle I had bought in Thamel a few days prior, I did the only thing I felt I had the power to do in the moment. I lit it and said a prayer to whoever and whatever could be listening.

"Please protect them," I asked. "Please watch over them."

I was awakened on my mat by the sensation of someone gently tapping my shoulder. "It is raining, ma'am, please come under the tarp." It was too dark to make out the face of who was speaking to me. Looking over my shoulder, I saw that many people were already under the covered awning, with maybe another thirty people or so anxiously attempting to squeeze in, laying their mats and blankets down in any free space and scooting the loungers and chairs like Tetris to make them all fit. I considered moving. I looked at the wall of the building next to me, for the hundredth time, surveying every neat line of red brick and appraising whether it would make it through the night standing. I considered moving my mat, but didn't want to leave the safety of my little trees or the prayer wheels. I'll stay. Ro, Joe, Dominique, and Inez made their way under the tarp, and for the first time, I was separated from my earthquake family.

The light rain started coming down a bit harder, and the sound of its patter lulled our group into semi-sleep. Out of the edge of my towel, I got a glimpse of the moon, peering out from beneath the blanket of clouds. Sleep somehow found me, bringing with it nightmares of cracking stone and fluid furniture. At some point deep in the night, a massive aftershock rolled through the valley, and I was awakened by the sound of people groaning as they tossed and turned, still half-sleeping, through the waves of movement underneath us, too tired, too exhausted, to get up or panic anymore. I tried to cover the exposed parts of my body with the towel, now quite wet, while sinking deeper into my mat. Slowly, I drowned in a sea of emotions, of outrage and grief. I was frightened, more scared than I had ever been in my lifetime. I wondered about all of the wonderful people I had met. I thought of the girls at the orphanage. *Where were they and were they safe? Were they sleeping safely under the trees outside their awful concrete prison of a home, or were they trapped? Who was there to comfort them?*

I crawled into an even smaller ball, the tiniest ball I could make, as if to disappear. Maybe if I am insignificant, like a fleck of dust, a crumb, a grain of sand, I won't be any trouble or burden for anyone here. I don't want to ask the world a thing—to take up any more space in the well of need and destruction that is right now, what was before, or what is to come. I don't want to add to what is already so wrong with it all. Maybe if I am small and quiet, I won't have to face it or be asked to fix it, because I don't know if I have the strength or power it takes to do so. I don't know what I have to offer it.

I was sucked deeper into a black vortex of the earth's pain, sensing it with every cell in my body. *I'm so sorry. I'm so sorry for what we have done.*

3

RELEASING
THE GRIP

"Nick, can you hear me?" I yelled to no avail. "Can you slow down a little?" I screamed, knowing my voice was drowned out by the sounds of the motor. The wind hit my face and body hard as we rode down the 101 freeway on the back of Nick's Triumph motorcycle; eighteen-wheelers rushed by on our right, an endless line of cars flew by on the left. I buried my head in his back, the air pushing so hard I felt like I was going to fall off.

Freeing his hand from the right handlebar, he reached back and patted my knee—his way of telling me, "It's OK, Momma—you are going to be just fine." I think back to our four-month family trip through Southeast Asia to establish GoPhil's NGO partners when Nick and Emma were in their early teens, how I had been too scared to drive the moped through the packed and crazy streets of Chiang Mai, Thailand. Nick, only fourteen at the time, had taken over for me. How quickly life was hurtling by.

I gripped his waist tighter as he moved across three lanes of dense traffic to exit for Malibu Canyon. It was our first ride together since he had purchased his motorcycle. Of course, John and I had our fears about letting him go through with it. Actually, I lie—that's an understatement. We had visions and nightmares of every possible horrible accident, the worst kinds; the ones you want to wake up from. But he was a man, with a right to make decisions for himself. He had visions for himself, and who were we to get in the way? Who were we to let our fears direct his future?

From the beginning, we had hoped to encourage the kids to dream big—to follow their passions, no matter what the world said around them. When we had left what appeared to be a perfect life in Orlando fifteen years earlier for a new life in the rural south of France, there had been no map, no set plan, no sure way to know where it was going to go. I distinctly remember my father warning me not to be so flippant about throwing away the financial security we had built for ourselves in such a short time with our consulting business. It's a natural response for a parent to fear and protect. But our six-year hiatus from the usual rat race in the US had allowed us the space to feel who we were inside, to hear the voices that spoke in a language of what made us happy. We wanted the kids to know their own language too.

Our eventual return to the US, however, had been bumpy— some of us in the family needed what was back at home more than others. After not earning a proper living since we had left the US six and a half years prior, John was eager to build something from years of learning about restoring old houses. We had created the beginnings of a villa rental agency during our years in Provence, which was increasingly becoming a popular tourist destination. He was keen to build a villa rental company, basing it out of the US as opposed to France, which we had learned was not an easy place to start, let alone grow a business. We moved back, settling in Rochester, New York. It was a familiar place—we had met there as teenagers. John's sister and her family lived in town, and it wasn't too far a drive from where our respective parents lived.

I had known from the start that we wouldn't remain in Rochester forever. Conversations about buying a house and truly committing to life there never really went anywhere. It was as if our lives were being lived outside of it—a life of comings and goings. The kids enjoyed being back in the US for the most part, but neither Nick nor Emma lasted long term in the traditional school system. After taking them out and homeschooling them during our extended trip through Southeast Asia to visit grassroots programs for GoPhil, Nick never returned to the typical classroom. He remained committed to his dream of becoming a recording artist, and that meant constructing his day around a different way of learning. Emma followed suit not long after, choosing to spend the cold upstate mornings riding and caring for horses. Both were enrolled in rigorous online distance learning programs, and they soon discovered we were not alone in living a life against the grain. We were amongst hundreds of other students and families who had chosen untraditional lifestyles—some lived on boats, some students were high-profile athletes who had intense training schedules, some were artists and musicians who required alternative school hours and a range of other flexible options. Others had enrolled in virtual school because they didn't thrive in an environment where conformity seemed to be a baseline to survival. Something was freeing about the kids having the space to define their own realities.

Nick's successful audition on Season 1 of *The X Factor USA* would guide our next move. He was recruited into a boyband and so we packed up our belongings and moved to Los Angeles where he could work daily with the group from a North Hollywood studio. Los Angeles seemed like a stark contrast to what we had sought when we had first moved back, but thankfully, we found much more to discover there than what people perceived on the surface.

I thought about all of this as Nick maneuvered the bike with ease, weaving our way into the cool canyons, past the Rock Store—famous for both bikers and celebrities off of Mulholland Highway. I felt more comfortable in my seat behind him now, letting go a little more with each bend in the road, more trusting of his movements and the flow of the bike. It was amazing how the smell of the earth and the mineral scents from the pavement made it up through the helmet. I was beginning to understand some of the thrill of riding—the physical connection to what was around you was unavoidable.

It had been a hard three years for Nick in LA—certainly not quite the shot into stardom he had hoped for since he was a child. As we climbed the mountain up to the Mulholland Snake, known for its breathtaking views and twisting, winding roads, I thought about how the music industry, like so many other businesses that revolved around money, fame, and influence, could be an ugly and unfair habitat to try and survive in, especially for someone so young. Kids like Nick, and thousands of them were trying to make it in the entertainment industry, had less tough skin at their ages, less ability to sift through the crippling judgment and criticism that came with it.

The road was taking a rather different direction from what he had pictured for himself as an individual artist and songwriter—one where he could express himself as he had wanted to. This would unfold later, and beautifully, in its own time. Eventually, the boyband project fell apart, and just like that—he felt his dreams were crushed and years of work were for nothing. No more studio, no more rigorous schedules, no more shows or music videos with Kylie Jenner. In the moment, the fall from such a high was overwhelming for him and for everyone around him to witness. He spent silent days in his room, quietly reliving all of the crazy and exciting moments.

And then an even stranger set of events began to unfold. Randy Phillips, one of the music industry's most influential men and the financial backer to the boyband, approached Nick to offer him a shot at a solo career. In the process, they stumbled onto some music Nick had produced for Emma. She, too, was a talented singer and songwriter, but had never sought the limelight as Nick had. Somewhat out of the blue, Emma was also offered an artist deal, with Nick producing her music, as he had always done for her. Slowly, though, the focus began to shift exclusively to Emma, and Nick felt sidelined. It was a rollercoaster of events that none of us quite knew what to do with.

The motorbike had a healing effect on him, as if it allowed him to reconnect to a part of himself that escaped all of the madness he was living. An unexpected thing had happened since buying it. He had been battling with acne, not just the odd pimple here and there, but some pretty bad stuff—which is not welcomed when you are being marketed as a boyband kid. Despite pressure from almost everyone to go on the strong antiviral drugs, he was committed to healing himself, in his own time. Amazingly, when he bought his Triumph, within weeks, if not days even, his face completely cleared. On the bike, there was no room for fear or for trying to imagine what the future would bring. There was only the peace and freedom of now.

As the wind continued to push around the contours of my body, I thought about the wonderfully rich yet strange mix of elements we had created in our lives as a family. It was a mess of homeschool, NGOs, and motorbikes. There were music contracts, shows with screaming teen girls, horses, and airports—a lot of them. There were stone houses, mistral winds, and poppy fields in Provence. Home had not been something we could touch and feel; it was what we felt in whatever space we occupied, at times together and at times apart. Our rather strange concept of home, for so many a normal and stable place, was not that way for us. But it was a safe somewhere where we allowed ourselves the space to imagine all that could be possible, for ourselves and for each other. Absolutely nothing was normal about it, but it was ours.

Tucking my face into Nick's warm back, I felt an intense rush of love for this beautiful being I had helped bring into the world. The feeling then spread to Emma and to Isabelle. I wanted, with every cell in my body, to hold on to this forever. *Grab it and don't let go.* How was I to possibly bear the weight of protecting my kids from the world and the lessons they needed to experience, and from the pain I knew they would no doubt face? *Was this my role?* I wondered. *In attempting to do this, would I be denying them the discovery of their own strengths and potentials?*

As we wound our way through the cool canyons, I could tell the music was flowing through Nick's brain by the way his helmet subtly swayed from side to side. I could hear a faint melody in between the wind and the motor. Somehow, in searching for his own escape from pain, my eighteen-year-old son was prepping me to do the same. I didn't know it yet, but I would be asked to trust that the kids had all they needed inside of them to navigate their path forward. I would learn the hard way that in fact, we all did.

4

LEAVING IT BEHIND

The vast wholeness of existence (the immeasurable,
multifaceted beauty of what it means to be human)
cannot be perceived through one life.

—Mallory Smith

THE MORNING SUN CAST arms of light across my mat. I heard a rustling around as people started to wake, many of them making their way to the generator where they had plugged in their phones. Soon everyone was focused on trying to connect to their loved ones. I sat up, rubbed my eyes, and attempted to retie my hair into an acceptable bun. While the sun was beginning to warm the patio, I felt cold and sticky.

I turned and took note of the woman who had been sleeping next to me. She looked German, or Dutch, with a cute short haircut. She was in her thirties, maybe. She reached over and grabbed the water bottle I had been given the night before; she took long, slow gulps, then handed it to the young man next to her. I wasn't sure what the water situation was going to be that morning, if it would become increasingly difficult to get more, but figured—*OK whatever—we will figure this out together. I'm OK to share.* She picked up her phone and motioned excitedly to her man friend—she must have service.

I thought of John, how worried he would be at this point. It had been almost twenty hours since the earthquake, and I was beyond anxious to make contact. A simple text letting him know I was fine would suffice at that point.

"Excuse me. Do you speak English?" I asked.

"Yes sure," she said.

"Do you think it might be possible to borrow your phone for one quick call or a text? I just want to let my husband and children know that I am OK."

She glanced down at the phone in her hand and then fumbled with it, looking uncomfortable.

"Is it to the US?" she asked with a concerned look on her face.

Wanting to avoid what I knew was going to be an awkward exchange, I responded quickly, "Yes, it is—no worries though. I'll see if I can find someone else."

A small knot formed in my stomach as I turned my back to her, disappointed. Maybe I would feel the same way—protective over the only links to a sense of security. I made my way, stepping over mats and people, some still sleeping, others folding their towels neatly as if they were preparing for their airplane to land after a flight, and found Dominique. Her smile and warmth comforted me right away. "Here," she said to me, handing me her phone. "Call home—the service is up."

I took the phone into my hands, grateful yet also impatient to make the call. I called John, but he did not answer. The sound of his voice on his message, so familiar yet so far, pierced my momentary sense of stability. I left what I now know was a scatty and emotional message that I was fine—separated from my passport and purse and with no shoes—but I would see about getting home once I assessed the situation. Before handing Dominique the phone, I thought of trying to reach Nick and Emma, but I couldn't for the life of me remember their phone numbers.

I made my way around to the pool and noticed that the staff had laid out a table with toothbrushes and other various toiletries. I took a toothbrush and approached the tap where a group had formed, and I joined the others as they scrubbed and spat. We looked at each other, acknowledging the strangeness of the moment. Here we were at a beautiful hotel, with broken windows, walls, and pots in crumbled heaps surrounding us, brushing our teeth next to each other.

Suddenly, the faint drone of a plane overhead reached our ears, and a surprised murmur spread throughout the crowd. Word circulated that the only planes coming in or out of the airport were Indian planes, coming to pick up their nationals, but it was still good news to know the airport was functioning. The owner of the hotel began making rounds, asking people about their return flights home. "There is a chance that some flights will be resuming," she said briskly. "Is anyone schedule to leave today?" My flight back to Delhi was due to leave that day—midday or 1 p.m., from my memory. My heart began to race, and I approached her, letting her know I was booked on a flight yet all of my things were still in the room. Would I be allowed to go in and retrieve them?

"We haven't let anyone in the rooms yet as it is too dangerous. You are sure you are on a flight today? What room are you in?" she asked.

"Room 25," I said.

"I'll send you up there with a porter. Get in and get out as quickly as you can. Come right back if you sense risk or you feel an aftershock." She motioned to one of her employees who quickly came to her side, then she explained in Nepali what we were to do. I looked at this young man, not much older than Nick, and wondered what he was thinking—why he had to risk his safety for some foreigner.

"Please—I can go alone," I told her, but she said this was the only way she would allow me to go.

Before there was time to contemplate further, he grabbed my arm, and we raced to the stairwell to my room. We stopped at the foot of the stairs, pausing briefly. I wondered if the stairs would hold, if they were still attached to each other. I wondered if our movement in the building would cause the floor or the walls to collapse. Then we ran up, skipping steps as we went. Upon reaching the landing, we entered the already opened door into the room.

Amazingly, my computer was still sitting on the desk, next to my backpack, as if nothing had happened. The room looked different, I didn't know how, yet also oddly the same, as if the whole thing had been a dream. I grabbed my things frantically while the porter zipped up my suitcase, which luckily had stayed packed. I made a quick scan of the bathroom, finding nothing, yet stopped to gaze at the small, square piece of handmade soap that sat next to the sink. I don't know if it was out of fear or desperation that I took it—perhaps it could be the last piece of soap I might see for days, or maybe I needed to take something solid, something, anything, from that room to remember that it had all been real.

We were back on the patio next to the pool in what felt like under thirty seconds. I could tell from the look in the porter's eyes and from the way he was panting that he had been as scared as I was. I grabbed his hands—"Namaste ... namaste," I repeated, as I attempted to relay my gratitude. Just then, a small smile crept across his face as if we had accomplished something in this mess. It was a brief second of control, a successful mission in a sea of madness. I think about this brave soul often, silently thanking him for accompanying me and wondering how he and his family fared. *Did he still work at Dwarika's? Had he been as scared as I had been going into that room?*

Finding a private place behind a potted plant, I took a moment to go through my things, to locate my passport, my phone, and the printout of my plane ticket. Air India 281, 12:50, April 26th, it read. I rummaged and found a pair of shoes to wear. I put on a new shirt. Even though the day was becoming hotter as the minutes passed, I wrapped myself up in my wool sweater. After zipping everything back up, I looked at the phone in my hand, expecting the batteries to be drained, but I was amazed to see it was at 75 percent. I called John and nearly melted to the ground as I heard his voice. He had awoken early that morning and, after hearing my voicemail, had immediately scoured the internet for news. His voice was calm, but I knew he was shaken. He was a patient and caring husband, allowing me to follow my passions in life, to travel around the world, oftentimes alone, finding special people and programs who were shouldering problems quietly and bravely as we went about our privileged lives. He had opened his heart and trusted me when I had crumpled at the age of twenty-seven, begging him to leave the normal life we had created for something else—something I couldn't explain but knew had to be discovered.

We didn't linger on the call. "Your hotel is only about a kilometer from the airport. Get yourself there and get on that plane to Delhi."

I found Inez, Dominique, Ro, and Joe sitting huddled in a group. None of them were due to fly, so they were making themselves comfortable, settling in for another day at the hotel. "I am going to try and make it to the airport," I said. "Who knows, though, I'll probably be back in a few hours."

We made sure we had one another's contact information and hugged each other goodbye. It was the first of many waves of guilt and grief I would feel for leaving. A big part of me wanted to stay, to help in some way, however small, in this terrible disaster.

The hotel owner had arranged a transport to take me to the airport and told me to go to the main entrance of the hotel to look out for it. I was expecting to see many others there and was surprised as only one other couple climbed in the van. They were clinging to each other, in their own worlds, nervous to get to the airport. As the van pulled away from the hotel, I glued myself to the window, anxious to see what had happened outside of the walls at Dwarika's.

We easily made our way down the length of the road that led to the airport; the road was normally bumper-jammed with traffic.

I noticed the green park was covered in tarps with hundreds of people huddled around small fires. The road appeared intact, as did most of the buildings. A lot of activity appeared to be taking place around the main Hindu temple area at Pashupatinath. Later, I learned that the hospitals had become so overcrowded that night that they had lined up beds along the riverbanks, and that over five hundred people had already been placed on burial pyres on the ghats, the stepped banks of the holy site and a sacred place to cremate bodies.

We arrived to sheer mayhem at the airport. Hordes of people stood waiting outside. The energy was tense and frenzied. People wandered around with bloody bandages on their heads and other parts of their bodies. Foreigners yelled angrily at officials who guarded the entrance doors; they were only letting in people who were booked on flights that were actually leaving, and only one had left that morning. I found a small, empty swatch of pavement and set my bag on it. Sitting on top of my bag, I settled in for what I thought could be a very long wait.

"Lydia—Lydia … how are you?" Shocked to hear my name, I turned to find the guide from Social Tours who had arranged some of my meetings with NGOs. "I have come to find you, knowing that you were on a flight today—I am trying to track down all of our clients to make sure they are fine and safe. Raj has spoken with your husband this morning." Raj, the founder of Social Tours, had met John at a trade show years before. Having similar values in the ethics surrounding "give back travel," they hit it off and we had stayed in touch ever since. When it was time for GoPhilanthropic to expand into Nepal, we called Raj right away.

Knowing all that was going on, all the groups he had to care for, especially those who had made their way to base camp, I was touched by their efforts to reach everyone. Steve Webster, another travel organizer, had made his way over to Dwarika's to do the same. I had stayed at Steve's lovely small boutique hotel in the hills surrounding Kathmandu a few days prior. He had introduced me to Dhorje and his vibrant little school in Dadaguan. I was shocked at the devotion they displayed to their clients at a time when their own families and employees were suffering terribly. Hard times were indeed ahead, yet in the moment, concern and care for others came first.

"Air India 281," an official yelled. "Passengers Air India 281, please come forward." I bolted up off my perch—*That's my flight! What are the odds?* I gathered my things as quickly as I could. About thirty people emerged from the heaving throngs, showing their passports and tickets to the officials. We stepped inside, and the doors shut behind us. Suddenly, as if out of a dream, the world became entirely silent and still. The arrivals check-in area was completely empty except for one airline employee, neatly dressed, standing behind the AirIndia desk. The whole scene was oddly surreal. Everything was clean and intact; the roof had not blown off as we had all imagined the night before. I have no recollection of going through security, though maybe I did in my daze. The rest of the airport was just as vacant. I bought some peanuts at the snack stand and sat with a handful of equally dumbfounded foreigners at the gate.

A few minutes later, we were guided onto the tarmac and waited under the midday sun to board the plane. When we did, nobody said a word. We arranged our bags and took our seats in silence without the normal commotion and fuss. Once settled into my seat at the back of the airplane, I looked up and noted that pretty much everyone was motionless, staring ahead, with little, if any, interaction with each other.

The plane began its forward motion, and before long we were tipped into the air. I didn't dare look to my left or right out of the windows. I didn't want to see what I knew was below me. Waves of grief and dread rushed up and down my body. And just when I thought the feelings were subsiding, a new one crept in, like a monster crawling out from underneath the bed, wrapping its long and bony fingers around my arm. Guilt was its name. *Why me? Why am I on this lucky plane running home? What makes me so special? Look at what I am leaving behind.*

5

CHANGING COURSE

Not all those who wander are lost.

—J.R.R. Tolkien

LANDING BACK IN NEW DELHI felt like I had arrived on another planet. In the airport, everyone moved around normally, the duty-free shop was full of customers, trendy Indian music played in the background, and the hum of coffee makers from the myriad of cafés and restaurants all blended into a swirl of real life—not the one I had just come from.

Delhi, and India in general, had become a constant in my life. I now knew the carpet on the New Delhi airport floor as if it were my own, and the smell in the air, the face full you get when the airplane doors open, had become wonderfully familiar. But for years, India had remained somewhat of a mystical place—a distant realm where my dreams were stored. Despite my lifelong passion for humanitarian work, I had hesitated to get involved as I approached my adulthood. I was accustomed to living with two distinct roadmaps inside my head. One was logical and spoke to me about the need for a "proper" career path; it made the best use of my education and provided the most security and tangible success. The other had a depth and power far greater than anything I could explain or measure and was driven by something more elusive. I kept that one stored away in my soul, protecting myself from it taking over; I knew good and well that if I let it, allowed it to take the wheel, I might never return to a "normal" life. And then I had a belief that if I kept to a more predictable, secure path, I might not be asked to do things I didn't have the strength to fix.

Despite my attempts to control these two dialogues, somewhere along the way, the lines began to cross. India had woven its way into these private conversations, and I was wise enough to know what team she belonged to. While living in France, we had traveled to a long list of places, but India never made it into the trip plans. Knowing that I was avoiding a place I had dreamed of visiting, John arranged for us to go for our tenth anniversary. Our days together are etched in my mind forever; I can still remember the smell in the air as the sun went down at the Taj Mahal and the sight of beautiful saris flapping gently in the wind in Rajasthan. India stole my heart, and the seal was broken. Within days of our return, I had booked another trip back to volunteer at an orphanage.

The experience was not at all what I had imagined, and it changed the course of my life. I had hoped to make a difference during my two-week stay, but I had fallen into an easy trap of thinking I could help vulnerable children in a country I wasn't familiar with, with little contextual knowledge or ability to communicate in their language. I returned home ashamed of my naive assumptions and motivated to understand how it could be done better. Enough was enough—I had been wandering around the world for the past six years. I had been shown enough of what was wrong with it. It was time to take action.

The concepts had been so basic at the outset—to find worthy people and programs and help to get them exposure through the influx of travelers to that region. I would create a person-to-person connection between the change-makers of the world who fought for basic needs and travelers who had a desire to give and share. I would make sure any contributions went directly to where they needed to go. It would be simple. Open the doors, create a flow of resources, then get out of the way.

But understanding the unique needs and priorities of people who struggled to survive in under-resourced areas, and facilitating personal connections for donors wanting to support their missions, would require way more thought and experience than I ever imagined. Luckily, after returning to the US from France, I joined forces with other bright, globally-minded women who would help navigate these complicated waters. Tracey Morrell and Linda DeWolf were also motivated to help strengthen grassroots programs in marginalized areas. Together, we expanded beyond my original concept of a socially conscious travel operation by creating GoPhilanthropic Foundation—an international grant-making organization. Our hope was to support the visions and dreams of small, locally-led and driven programs. By combining funding, capacity-building, and networking, we could help provide them a bigger platform to do what they were already doing well. In our first five years, we had forged partnerships with over twenty-five NGOs in Southeast Asia, Africa, and India, working on gaining access to education, health, and human rights. By 2020, this would double.

The work required to build GoPhil had been my teachers and guides—offering me difficult, at times frustrating, life coursework in what it meant to make a difference, to play a truly useful role in contributing to solutions to global problems. What had seemed so simple at the beginning—finding money and getting it to people in need—was developing into a much richer tapestry. In listening more and more to the people and programs we partnered with, we realized their dreams, and maybe our mission, had less to do with collecting handouts for them from donors, and more to do with helping them rewire the systems that had unjustly left them out from the start. We would realize over the years that money was only one form of currency that was needed to solve complex problems and that "people in need" were far from being "poor." If we entered into the dialogue assuming we knew more because we had more financial resources, we were already off on the wrong foot.

GoPhil now had close and longstanding relationships in India with several small community-led programs doing important work with at-risk women and children, and many of those relationships had begun in Delhi. We had been providing desperately needed support at the SMS Center for children who were growing up on the infamous GB Road, the second largest red-light district in the world. We partnered with TARA Child Protection who provided an important alternative to the systematic institutionalization of children that was becoming widespread in India. We had locked arms with Shakti Shalini, a program fighting gender-based violence, started by two mothers who joined forces after their young daughters were burned alive by their in-laws due to insufficient dowries.

Walking through the airport, I knew I was in no state to visit with these special colleagues, people who, over the years, had become my close friends. I wasn't in a place where I could listen to the difficult challenges they faced every day. I needed to get to a hotel, take a bath, and find a way home to Los Angeles. I got into a taxi and within five minutes was walking into the cool marbled lobby of a hotel. With every step I took toward the check-in counter, I felt more and more separated from what I had just experienced. Looking back, it is clear as day that I was far from being in a normal state of mind, that post-traumatic stress had begun to take hold, but none of this was evident to me in the moment, nor would it be for some time.

Taking the elevator up to the third floor was a terrifying experience; I couldn't distinguish the movement under my feet with the feeling of the rolling earth underneath me. And once in the room, everything moved in slow motion. I put down my bags and got on all fours, feeling the plush cream carpet between my fingers. I rested there for a bit and then made my way to the bathroom, peeling off my dirty clothes as I went. I soaked for a long time in the bath, scrubbing my body raw with the loofah and washing my hair multiple times. I stared at the small bar of soap I had taken out from my bag and placed on the bathroom counter, the one from my room at Dwarika's. I felt my heart tug as I wondered what everyone there was doing at that moment, what the country would have to face in the coming days and months.

I called the airlines and told the representative that I had been in the earthquake in Nepal—could they waive the change fees due to the circumstances and get me home that night? I was surprised when the woman told me she hadn't been aware of any earthquake. "Can I put you on hold, Mrs. Dean?" she said politely. "I will just check in with my supervisor." When she returned, she was armed with the latest news and was more than accommodating in putting me on a flight that evening through Amsterdam.

Knowing that the Delhi airport officials required a printout of your ticket to enter the airport, I made my way to the business center. This, unfortunately, required another trip in the elevator. *Two floors, Lydia, it's only two floors.* But within minutes of feeling the light shaking of the elevator as it made its way up, I felt my heart rate skyrocket. When the doors reopened, I ran to the business center desk. "The buildings are going to come down—listen to me—I feel an earthquake, we need to get out," I pleaded. It wasn't until I looked into the employee's eyes and saw the concern washing over his face that I realized I might not be right—that my body was still functioning in a state of high alert.

"No ma'am, I think the building is fine," he said, guiding me gently to a chair. The staff in the business center were surprised to learn that I had just come from Kathmandu that afternoon. "The airport is now closed. They had a massive 6.7 aftershock right before 1 p.m."

Good god. I rushed back to my room, still unsteady on my feet, but in a sheer panic to get to my computer to learn about the aftershock, to get any news I could about what the damage. I found a link online which described the aftershock as hitting only minutes after my plane had left, sending massive rolling tremors through the airport, forcing airport staff, officials, and travelers to run for cover as the building shook violently. All flights had stopped afterward.

Pascal, the director at TARA, stopped by the hotel. I had texted him earlier in the day, explaining what had transpired and that we would not be meeting. Pascal and I had become good friends over the years, and he must have picked up on the anxiety in my voice. "Have a nap. You need sleep, and I'll make my way over." I tried to sleep, but my heart continued to beat a mile a minute. When he arrived, we caught up for a bit, but I had trouble holding a normal conversation. "Lyd—you need a warm massage, anything to get you out of this state of panic." *A massage? This isn't the moment for indulgent and unnecessary pampering*, I thought, but looking back, he was right. I needed to begin to release what was tightening inside. I remember two things about the massage—one was the constant stream of tears, without emotion, that rolled out from my eyes. And the other was shaking uncontrollably. I simply could not find warmth.

A few hours later, I made my way to the Delhi airport, heading directly to the lounge to wait out the hours before the flight. Feeling lightheaded, I realized I hadn't eaten in a long time. In fact, I couldn't remember my last real meal. I tried to piece together a chronology of the past days, attempting to land on a concrete day and time, a breakfast or lunch, something, but I got confused and gave up. I got up and scanned the buffet for something warm and comforting. It included a mixture of curries but none of them appealed to me—the meat looked oily and the vegetables tired. I resorted to a bag of chips and a glass of wine. It turned into two. I needed to ensure sleep, I told myself.

Once on the plane from Delhi to Amsterdam, I passed out soundly for the first time in days, waking just as we were landing. I gazed over to the man sitting next to me who was deep into an article in the paper about the earthquake. I stared at the pictures in disbelief, of people crawling out of the rubble, bodies piled up by the sides of the torn-up roads. Chills ran up and down my body, but the frigid sensation didn't stop after a few seconds as I had expected it to. The cold sunk deep into my insides, as if freezing my organs, one by one.

As the plane's wheels hit the tarmac, a thought then took hold. *I'm probably the first person to be returning to Los Angeles from Nepal. I need to get the word out. I have to get the money flowing, and there is no time to lose.* During my short connection, I called John to let him know I wanted him to contact all of the local TV stations. "We have to move on this now before it's not news anymore. Line them up—we need to do this quickly," I insisted. For the next ten hours on the following flight, I scrambled to get all of my notes together from my trip, carefully documenting all of the people and organizations I had met, knowing that they would need help immediately. By the time I reached the section describing the girls I believed to be trapped in the shelter home in Dhulikhel, I had a painful lump in my throat. My heart raced and my mind ran in circles thinking of the best next steps to take. We would need to send out an immediate appeal to our donors. They would react quickly, I was sure. I just knew they would help.

As I was scanning my notes, I saw three words scribbled on the side of my journal. I vaguely remembered jotting down the words before falling asleep on the last flight:

PLAY, GRACE, and CLARITY.

And then I remembered. Sometime as night was falling at Dwarika's, Inez had pulled out a miniature tarot deck of cards from a little pouch in her purse. I had become quite fascinated with reading tarot and oracle cards, so I noticed right away that it wasn't a typical tarot deck. On each card was a symbol and written beneath it, a single word. "Let's each pull some," she had said. "To pass the time. Maybe there is some deep meaning in all of the madness." We each went around and took three cards, turning them over carefully. PLAY, GRACE, and CLARITY, mine had said. Knowing I was not in a place to process much, I simply made a mental note of them.

My stomach dropped as the plane made its descent—I continued to stare at the words, taking deep breaths as if to ingest each one of them individually, to bring them inside of me. While I couldn't draw any meaning from them yet, I knew they held important messages. I closed my notebook, then my eyes, and my mind went blank for the remaining few minutes before landing.

John was waiting for me at the airport at the foot of the escalator at baggage claim, wearing his go-green T-shirt, a favorite of mine, and white pants. It's five years later as I write this, yet I remember his outfit distinctly. It was fresh and clean and predictable, and I fell into his arms, his safe, strong, and capable arms. I wanted to cry, to melt, to drop to my knees in relief of it all being over, but the tears didn't come. Only another chill up my spine. "Don't get too close to me," he said, pulling away. "I was up all night with a stomach flu or something. It came on out of the blue. I feel like hell." Looking at him more closely, I noticed how drained he looked, and it dawned on me how powerless he must have felt being so far away from the situation.

"Did you call the news stations?" I asked impatiently as we walked to the car. "No Lyd—I didn't. It all sounded a bit crazy. Don't you want to just breathe a minute? Can that wait a day or two?"

"No, it can't," I said, hearing the hint of impatience in my own voice. "You don't understand—it has to be now. Nobody is going to care in a few days." I was beside myself with frustration, anxious to get home and start making calls. I didn't say much for the remainder of the drive—it felt endless, and I was nauseous from the long journey and the stop-and-go, bumper-to-bumper traffic. When we were finally home, John got my bag from the back of the car while I entered the house. He knew that what I wanted more than anything was to see the kids, to smell their skin, run my hands through their hair, feel the warmth from the bodies I knew so well. I made my way around the house to greet each one. They acted a little strange with me, each in their own way, as if they didn't know what to say or do—not knowing whether to bring up the events of the past days, to ask questions, or to just leave it alone.

After a quick shower, I made a series of calls to local news outlets, and two TV stations came to the house for interviews later that day. In any normal situation, I would have been consumed by nerves at the thought of being on television, but I was simply numb to it all. I described the experience as I had remembered it and made a simple plea for help. Nepal would need every bit of help it could get; every penny was going to count.

That night as the house settled down and John and the kids each slipped into their rooms to go to sleep, I allowed myself my first breath of relief at being home. It felt good—so safe and familiar—yet at the same time, I couldn't quite reach the comfort I was seeking. Something had shifted deep inside of me, and I was a long way from coming to terms with what that meant.

As I made my way up to bed, I noticed a fortune cookie on the ledge above the kitchen sink. They must have ordered Chinese food while I was gone. If a family member was not present at the meal, we would save them their cookie to open later. I cracked it open and read the message. "Your life will change course in the coming months," it said.

Nearly nine thousand people died and more than twenty-two thousand suffered injuries during the April 25, 2015, earthquake that measured a magnitude of 7.8. It was the deadliest earthquake in the seismically active region in eighty-one years.

It affected 3.5 million people (about a third of the national population). More than six hundred thousand homes were destroyed and more than 288,000 were damaged. The strongest impact was felt in remote rural areas, where people were and continue to be the most vulnerable.

6

NEW NORMAL

What you think you are is a belief to be undone.

—A Course in Miracles

THE FOLLOWING WEEKS CREPT BY, day by painful day. It was as if time had slowed down and everything in my usual backdrop to life felt entirely different, like a filter had been placed over my field of vision, or that the composition of the air had been reconstructed. The literal makeup of my body even felt new to me. But something else was at work, and it had to do with this conversation between the earth and sky that had come to mind when I was looking at the prayer wheels at Dwarika's. I didn't know how to begin to decipher what it was saying at the time; I was too confused and scared, yet during the coming months and years, I would get glimpses of understanding into what it was saying, and perhaps what I was meant to be learning.

But as I had experienced in earlier years when I had a hunch that I had to find something that was out there, I would have to follow a crumb path, at times in the dark and alone, to get from one lesson, one classroom, to the next.

My desire to be a good mother and my devotion to GoPhilanthropic had both come from a deep desire to help others find and expand their greatness—and so far, I felt I had done a decent job. But within that mission, I was also being forced to find the best in myself, and for some reason, that concept was terrifying, like climbing Mount Everest with no shoes. Later—much later, these amazing discoveries would help me come to terms with how my own healing was essential in trying to make whole an imperfect, imbalanced, yet beautiful world out there. This next life coursework would force me to acknowledge that giving to myself was a vital, essential part of being able to give to others, that healing the world begins within ourselves. But those first days back from Nepal were only the beginning of a long road to truly understanding this.

The days following my return to LA started with the grueling task of getting out of bed after nights of sleep that went somewhere deeper than normal, but they were almost always accompanied by dreams, mostly nightmares that took me back to Nepal. In the mornings, I often laid motionless before getting out of bed, staring at the two large pine trees outside my bedroom window. *How is it that I never really noticed these beautiful beings before?* I studied each one of them, admiring their strong and calming presence, fascinated by their quiet determination. I wasn't sure what they could be reaching for up in that blue sky, if anything at all, but I was sure that they were worthy of great respect. Some days I imagined the two trees to be having conversations with each other—soulful chats about all sorts of things that we probably didn't give a moment's notice to as we buzzed around senselessly beneath them. I would then wait patiently for the sun to make its way to a particular spot that cast bright and powerful rays on its branches before making my way downstairs.

Some days I would get up in time to walk Isabelle the two blocks to Nestle Elementary School. When we had arrived in Los Angeles, we had scoured the region for the best schools. We decided on a small, private one in Woodland Hills. It was a bit of a drive and more than we had wanted to pay, but we hadn't heard positive things about the public school system. A year later, when Izzy failed to show any interest in school whatsoever, we began to question the price and the pretense that came along with the smart uniform. Throwing caution to the wind, we enrolled her in the local public school only a few minutes' walk from our house. The school yard was dotted with small, portable classrooms and was surrounded by an old chain-link fence—not an impressive-looking place by any means, but within a few months, Isabelle showed signs of interest in learning again, enjoying the diversity of students who came from a wide range of backgrounds and countries. And maybe somewhere in her mind, she also enjoyed knowing that we were close by, only a few houses away.

My morning walks with Isabelle were different after returning from Nepal. Before, I would have been showered and ready for the day, coffee in hand. I might have tried to fill the minutes of our walk with questions, attempting to get brief access into a world she often kept private. But now, lacking my normal energy, I didn't even glance in the mirror to tidy up my hair, let alone get out of my pajamas. I was just happy to walk next to her, to feel the morning breeze on my skin, to not care about stepping on the pavement cracks. On my way back, I would attempt to prepare myself for the day ahead—to try as best I could to reclaim some of the normalcy from before.

I tried to find an escape from my new, foreign state of mind through my usual workout routines. Running had been my life-long friend, an outlet that had seen me through all my life's twists, turns, and hiccups, and we had access to a fantastic network of canyon trails up Reseda Boulevard, only a five-minute drive from our house. I would typically lose track of time on those cracked earthy paths, which reminded me so often of the trails near our house in Provence. But I just didn't seem to have the energy to last more than thirty minutes. And the sun felt so hot. Just too hot.

Emma dragged me to one of her spinning classes; it ended in total disaster. The dark room, loud music, and intensity of so many bodies frantically spinning on their bike seats had me escaping to the bathroom within minutes of class starting. Thinking I needed a gentler form of exercise, John encouraged me to return to yoga with him—we were both enrolled at the local Yogaworks studio and he was sure it would be exactly what I needed. For a while, it seemed to help. The bare, cool walls and empty clean spaces were calming. The sound of breathing and the hum of the air conditioner would lull me into a deep resting space. At times during the class, waves of emotion washed over me, always accompanied by chills running through me, up and down my body. I thought this might be healthy, that the toxic stress of the experience was making its way out of me. Yoga was working, I thought. But more and more with each pose, I felt confronted with a requirement to bend that I was simply unable to face—I felt I was resisting in every pose. I had lost trust in the floor, in my mat, and in myself. After a week or two of returning to class, my back seized and that was the end of that.

With no clear physical escape routes, my mind found other ways to try to put life back into predictable order. I spent days cleaning, throwing out anything that seemed unimportant or unnecessary and arranging things neatly in drawers. One Saturday afternoon, Emma walked into my closet where I had spent most of the day amidst heaps of clothing that I was re-hanging in meticulous, color-coordinated uniformity. "Mom ... what are you doing? When have you ever cared about organizing your clothes like this. What's going on?" she asked, a little concerned. Looking up at her, and then over to the rows of clothes perfectly arranged from one end of my closet to the other by shade and tone. "I don't know babe—it just seemed like the natural thing to do."

But one particularly disturbing experience during those initial weeks topped all others at the time. I wasn't enjoying making dinner each evening for the family as I always had. The thought and effort that went into the planning, shopping, and cooking felt like an insurmountable set of tasks. As a result, we were ordering out or eating out much more often than we normally did.

"Hon—how about you and I steal away for a light bite at Emilio's tonight," John suggested one evening. With three children and Nick and Emma both homeschooled, time alone, to ourselves, was a rare thing. "Sure. That sounds really nice." Emilio's was a favorite spot of ours on Ventura Boulevard in Encino—a simple, family-run Italian place with great food and no fuss. I was pleased when we were seated in a quiet far corner of the restaurant, next to a giant, three-foot geranium. When our salads and wine had been delivered, we did what we would normally do in our private time together, reviewing in detail what was going on with each of the kids, one by one, then moving to the Only Provence Villa business, and then to the Foundation. These were our life buckets, things we had helped to birth and people we cared for, tended, and watched grow each day.

I didn't know if it was the wine going to my head or just that I was tired, but suddenly I felt swimmy—and overcome with emotion. But the bizarre thing was that it wasn't just one emotion, it was a whole range of them and in no particular order. In a matter of minutes, I was consumed with frustration, then anger, then I felt as if I wanted to laugh. And I was drawn to what was happening at each of the tables around us—in fact, my focus was moving methodically from one to the next.

"Lyd—are you in there? Why are you staring at everyone? What is going on with you?" John said impatiently. My eyes stopped on the table nearest to us where a couple was speaking softly. I couldn't hear them, but they appeared to be in a serious, intimate discussion. Then all of a sudden, I felt very, very sad and was overcome with the urge to cry. Noticing my eyes filling with tears, John reached for my hand. "Lyd, what's wrong with you? Talk to me, honey. What are you thinking?"

It then became clear what was happening to me, yet I couldn't come to terms with it, let alone describe it. I felt as though I was picking up on every emotion in the room, on what people were feeling in their respective conversations. It was an incredibly intense experience to sense the various energies in the room and not have any control over it. It was like the boundary, the invisible walls that divide us as living beings and what we feel inside, simply ceased to exist. I felt part of them, as if we were no longer distinguishable, as if we weren't separate. It was disturbing and frightening, and I just wanted it to stop. "John, get me out of here," I begged. "Just take me home. I don't know what is happening to me. I must be having a nervous breakdown."

Once in the car, I started to replay the events in my head, and the words came tumbling out in between sobs. "What the hell just happened in there, John? Something is totally wrong with me. I swear to god, I could feel stuff in there that wasn't mine. Those weren't my feelings, and they kept changing from one table to another. I think I am going crazy—I really do. I don't know who I am anymore. I just want to feel normal again," I cried.

At the time, it didn't occur to either one of us that I might be experiencing the effects of PTSD (post-traumatic stress disorder). In my mind, that happened to people who were exposed to war, serious accidents, or violent assaults. But the minute I began to process the extent of the pain and loss others were experiencing as a result of the earthquake, I set about minimizing what was going on internally within myself. I could leave. I was home. I was safe and sound while others, people who were already facing extreme economic and social injustices, were left to face the aftermath. The guilt of my privilege, something I had been born into yet had never asked for, had perhaps been the thorny catalyst to wanting to fight for the rights of those who were denied them.

John was incredibly caring and patient with me, listening to everything I said yet not reacting too much. He took the long way home, weaving up the shady, tree-lined roads in the hills above Ventura Boulevard, giving me time and space to let it all out, to express something I had no words yet to explain. It was the first big cry, the most significant release I had since being back. I could tell he was quietly taking note of the changes he was seeing in me but not wanting to make me feel conscious of them. As he has done so often in our lives as a couple, he accepted where I was, and did not demand much more. All I knew was that up until the moment in that hotel room in Kathmandu when the water bottles toppled over, life had made sense. I had married the man of my dreams and had three beautiful children. We had followed our dreams, traveled the world, and built a life and a business in Provence. And after endless years of wondering how I could share some of what I believed I had unfairly been given too much of, we had created GoPhil. All of this was everything I had ever wanted, and while it was still there in front of me, untouched, the ground beneath it had moved.

7

DRY GROUND

We have two glorious tasks; to be a good steward to the gift
we are given and to wait upon that gift.

—Michael Jones

SOMETIMES BEFORE STARTING MY WORKDAY, I
would take my coffee out into the backyard and let the sun warm
my face. Our yard in Los Angeles wasn't like any I had grown up
with as a child in Canada, or as a teen in upstate New York where
lawns were vast, and it took you all weekend to mow or rake the
fall leaves. I spent my childhood running barefoot across them,
from one house to another, returning home with black-bottomed
feet that I would try to hide from my mother as I crawled into bed,
hoping she wouldn't notice. Our LA yard was also a far cry from
the rolling vineyards and herb-studded fields and wildflowers we
had grown accustomed to in Provence. It was a new experience
altogether, made up of a swatch of coarse green grass that felt more

like blades under your bare feet. It was entirely walled in, so you couldn't see past fifty feet in any direction, and power lines criss-crossed the blue skies above us. Beyond the bit of green, most of the space consisted of concrete that surrounded a very small pool—so tiny you could swim the length of it in one lap.

But what it might have lacked in acreage and greenery, it made up for in other ways. Birds came and went throughout the day from the outstretched arms of my new towering pine friends, and there was a fantastic Meyer lemon tree that leaned over the fence into our space from the opposite house. I didn't realize it yet, but the bounties of my backyard were only just opening up to me.

Feeling a little anxious one morning, I found myself walking around with my coffee, staring at the skinny space that divided our house and the neighbor's. It was so small you could almost stand arms outstretched and touch both houses. Along the edge of the thin sidewalk that ran the length between our houses was a strip of earth—a dried-up, weedy flower bed that sat lifeless for the three years we had rented the house, and probably the renters before us. Being as busy as we were, my taking trips to Asia, the activity with Nick, and now Emma's music, and still returning to France several times a year—I hadn't even noticed it, hadn't given thought to what else it could do.

As if out of a dream, a vision developed before me of this lifeless, dry ground transforming into a lush and verdant Eden, with vegeta-bles of all kinds pushing their way through the ground and up the concrete wall. I pictured juicy tomatoes, eggplant, zucchini, and swiss chard. *Look at all of this magnificent space.* All I could think of was getting my hands deep into the earth, to feel its warmth and goodness, to give life, to make something from the thirsty, cracked soil that had the natural potential to do so much more. But before another image of a fresh vegetable could surface, fear crept through my consciousness. I had never grown a thing; I had, in fact, killed many a houseplant. My mother is a fantastic gardener, growing everything from spring lettuce to three-foot sunflowers. Growing up, she was the image of joy in her sun hat, trowel in hand, on cloud nine passing entire days under the hot summer sun in her cottage house outside of Toronto. But I wasn't like her, and there was a very real possibility that I could fail miserably at this. I was OK to take other risks, but this seemingly manageable project, at that moment in time, seemed almost crazy.

But something inside of me took hold, a force that was stronger than anything I could fear, and right then and there, I decided to tackle this immense goal. I needed this dry strip of earth, and she needed me. I was bursting to tell John and the kids of this brilliant idea. I turned and made my way back into the house, slopping my coffee everywhere, to share the fantastic news. Nick and Emma were milling around the kitchen making breakfast, and John was at the table deep into his email, his Provence workday already nine hours ahead of him with the time zone difference. "You guys, listen up. I have the greatest plan—you're going to love it," I said, beaming ear to ear. Everyone stopped what they were doing to listen as I hadn't shown this much energy or joy in some time.

I don't know what they were expecting, maybe that I had a plan to go on a trip or to trade in our Hyundai for something more exciting, but I am certain they weren't expecting me to say what I came out with.

"Are you ready? I think we should transform the side area over there between the house and the neighbor's house into a vegetable garden. Wouldn't it be over the top to grow our own food? Wouldn't it be great to go out and pick our own lettuce for salads every night? Can you even imagine?" I screeched, almost laughing at the outrageousness of the thought.

John stopped typing, briefly glanced up at me, then returned to his email. Nick raised his forehead in bewilderment—"Ha ... Ma ... I thought you were going to come out with something good," he chuckled as he skipped upstairs to his bedroom. Emma rolled her eyes and went back to buttering her toast. "Uh yeah, Mom—would be great."

I was pretty deflated for a brief second, but the concept was so right to me, it represented such a simple, essential need at the time, that I carried on with my high. I rushed right upstairs to my room and called my sister Helene in England. I told her about my idea with the same level of enthusiasm, also admitting that I was actually really—*no very*— intimated by the thought. She listened patiently, no doubt a little surprised by my overreaction to such a basic plan coupled by a shocking lack of confidence. Big sisters have a way of summing things up succinctly. "Lyd—any idiot can grow a tomato," she said flatly.

For the next few days, I did nothing but watch YouTube videos for the beginner gardener. *This looks doable. It actually looks kind of easy.* Ready to sink my hands into the ground, I made my way over to the garden store. I grabbed a flatbed cart and gingerly walked up and down the aisles, like I do at times in foreign grocery stores when I travel, peering at shelves filled with strange and unknown things. I surveyed each and every row of plants as if they were miniature aliens, marveling at their different leaves; some had little blossoms that I knew from watching videos were the beginnings of a vegetable.

Gosh, where to start? And what if they each need different things to grow? What if they are like Nick, Em, and Iz—each completely different from one another? Nick would seek attention 24/7 while Emma avoided it like the plague, preferring not to be touched. Isabelle required all of the above, but you had to guess when, and I usually got it wrong. Then I remembered what worked across the board for each one of them, the common denominators that never failed me. Food and love. *OK I can figure this out. Let's just get on with this.*

I filled my cart with little plants, carefully placing them one by one in my cart. At the checkout, I realized I didn't have any gardening tools. Not knowing what I would need, I found a trowel—*that looked useful*—and a pair of gardening gloves, and called it a day.

I drove fast all the way home, thinking of nothing other than my rich and bountiful garden-to-be. Looking back, I was nothing short of obsessed. I reversed into the driveway and opened the side gate that led to the line of earth between our house and the neighbor's, unloading the plants from the car, placing each one on the sidewalk near where I thought it could go. *Welcome to your new home, guys. It's a fresh start, and I am your mother.* I beamed.

Now time to prepare the soil. I rummaged through the garage and found the shovel that had gathered dust behind a row of boxes. Back at my strip of earth, I began to dig, attempting to create the heaping dark clumps of earth I knew my babies needed, but the shovel didn't make it more than an inch into the dirt. Must be a rock or something underneath. I tried another spot, and then another, but there was little movement. *This isn't fun.* After about four minutes, I sat down on the sidewalk, sweating and totally winded.

Besides the frustration of feeling utterly inept at digging a simple, small hole in the dry LA ground, I had started to notice that alongside a general lack of energy, I was feeling a growing ache across my torso. At times, the sensation developed into a deeper pain that seemed to spread everywhere across my body. And to top it off, my right arm and thumb had begun to tingle and feel numb. I was successful most days in ignoring the pain, denying its presence, but as the weeks wore on, it only expanded and intensified. And none of this helped in turning over this hard, lifeless soil.

I sat ruminating over what I knew I had to do, but didn't want to accept. *Fuck—I need John. I can't do this myself.* Accepting defeat, I stumbled into the house and found him at the computer. "Hon— can you come and help me dig? I just can't do it. I just don't have the energy," I said, not wanting to admit the bit about the searing pain that was running through the lower half of my body.

"Sure," he said quickly—as if he was waiting for me to ask. "Let me just throw on some shorts."

I will never, ever forget a minute of what transpired in the following hours. Knowing I wanted to be part of every step of the transformation, John pulled up a chair near the patch where the garden would be and plunked me in it. He then proceeded to turn over the dry, cracked earth using the shovel with big sweeping competent scoops, one after another. I sat there and admired how his muscles moved gracefully, as if it was the most natural thing in the world to do. Then he carefully mixed in the potting soil the guy at the garden place had suggested I buy for extra nutrients. I watched as he took the time needed to make sure it was thoroughly blended. Knowing myself, I probably would have rushed that part. But John had this way of doing things properly, respecting whatever was required to genuinely complete a task.

When the earth was ready, he turned back to me curled up in the chair. "Do you want to put the plants in?" he asked gently. Consumed by what was now full-body pain, I couldn't imagine bending over. The thought made me want to be sick. "No, go ahead," I gestured. I watched him as he laid each one in its new bed, watering them gently afterward. I sat up and admired our new garden. While it was still in its infancy, it was everything I needed at the moment. It was hopeful—the opposite of everything I had just witnessed in Nepal. It was the very first step in making amends with the earth that I hadn't respected or expected could get so angry.

While I was disappointed that I hadn't been able to do it myself, John had managed to make me feel as though I had. He had taken what was in my heart and prepared a space for it to grow. In doing so, he reminded me of the beauty and significance that can reside in the simple acts of caring for one another, and I couldn't have loved him any more for it.

8

FORGING ON

Humankind has not woven the web of life. We are but one
thread within it. Whatever we do to the web, we do to ourselves.
All things are bound together. All things connect.

—Chief Seattle

DESPITE ALL OF MY NEW ECCENTRICITIES, one
part of my life had stayed constant. It was not in slow motion, painful, or blocked in any way, and that was my work with GoPhil. While
our partnerships spanned seven countries at the time, I focused my
attention entirely on Nepal, staying in close touch with the people
and programs I had met on the trip and continuing to raise funds
while it was still on the world's radar. Linda and Tracey, GoPhil's two
other co-founders, had suggested I take some time to ease back into
work, warning me about diving into our typically heavy days that
required staying in regular communication with the programs we
supported and sharing this frontline information with our active

community of donors. They sensed the extent of my fragility as the weeks unfolded, and I hadn't quite returned to my normal self.

"Lydia—it's probably best to take stock of how you feel—take it easy, maybe take a couple of weeks off. We can handle this," they urged. Deep down I knew they were right, but it didn't feel like an option. "I know this seems crazy, but it's the only activity that feels right at the moment. The only thing that seems normal to me is to do something tangible in the face of this tragedy," I explained.

It had been almost four years that we had worked together, the three of us combining our passions and devoting every possible minute to building what we believed was bringing together two sacred threads. One thread signified the people and programs doing important justice work in their underserved communities, and the other represented global citizens who wanted to share their resources, to do more than write a check, and connect with the world on a deeper level. Our jobs were to do whatever we could to ensure a safe space where this could happen.

Our portfolio centered specifically around NGOs offering access to education, health, and human rights. In Kenya, we worked with founder Helen Nkuriaya, who rescued girls from female circumcision and early marriage. Our partners in Guatemala, such as ASSADE and Centro Maya, were working on providing critical health care services within under-resourced Mayan communities. In Southeast Asia, we supported small, innovative education programs and family-strengthening and anti-trafficking efforts. In India, we worked with a host of programs primarily relating to gender inequality, trafficking, and child labor. Our work in Nepal was only just beginning to unfold but would later become the region where we piloted a "seed grant," program, encouraging small NGOs to collaborate on projects together as opposed to working in silos. In all cases, we aimed to invest in the potential that already existed within these initiatives, to help our partners realize their dreams for a more fair future.

GoPhil provided grants to fund the most critical needs based on the partners' priorities, and we had approximately twenty to thirty ongoing grants at any time. In many cases, we funded the most unattractive line items, yet fundamentally important elements on a small organization's budget. These ranged from funding salaries or training for qualified staff, to basic operational costs such as electricity and internet services. Donors traditionally wanted to invest in more measurable, trackable items, like class-rooms, books, or other tangible materials that they felt showed clearer, more direct impact from their funds. But more and more, we were moving in the opposite direction, seeing the importance of allowing flexibility in where the funds flowed, trusting that the programs knew best what they needed.

I am often asked if working in the development sector is sad—if it is hard to see the scale and results of widespread poverty and marginalization. My experience has been the furthest thing from depressing. If I could scream one thing far and wide, it would be that working alongside grassroots community leaders and change-makers, the oftentimes unsung heroes of social justice and true humanitarians, has been nothing short of hopeful, humbling, and awe-inspiring. Learning from them has been the single biggest example of just how resourceful, creative, and compassionate human beings can be. Once our little team at GoPhil began to see that our partnerships helped, even in small ways, to expand on this hope, there was no stopping us.

Linda would fundraise to anyone who was willing to listen to her, while Tracey built the back-end donor operations and finances. I did the research to find the programs alongside developing GoPhilanthropic Travel's journeys where people could meet them face to face. We all traveled a lot, and we all worked way too much. With three children each still in our nests, Tracey and I spun our plates full time, robbing Peter to pay Paul when it came to splitting time between our families and GoPhil. Running GoPhil was incredibly rewarding for each of us, but it also meant a sacrifice. The focus on others became our full-time existence, and one in which caring for ourselves often ended up last on the priority list. We would eventually face the consequences of this grave miscalculation, each in our own personal way. Not only was it counterproductive at times, but it represented what I now believe to be an outdated, limited assumption that giving needs to be a selfless act.

In the weeks following the earthquake, I scrolled Facebook for updates from Raj at Social Tours and from Steve Webster at Escape2Nepal; they were no longer running travel companies but instead leveraging their extensive networks and connections across the country, facilitating relief in villages that were not being reached by the larger aid agencies. They were able to do all of this while surrounded by friends and family who had not only lost their homes and livelihoods, but in some cases, whose wives, toddlers, brothers, and mothers were still missing.

Dealing with the massive earthquake was a new situation for all of us at the foundation. We hadn't had experience with any emergency disaster before, and we had to make critical decisions quickly and nimbly. We also recognized that our lack of experience required that we stay out of the way in some respects, allowing the berth needed for larger organizations who were more skilled in disaster situations to work more effectively on a large scale.

There was much to learn from the corruption that emerged after the devastating earthquake that hit Haiti in 2010 and left 220,000 people dead, three hundred thousand injured, and rubble as far as the eye could see. The $13.5 billion in international aid that flowed into the country is argued to have had some destructive effects on Haiti, despite the good intentions of donors and aid agencies. And the catastrophe unleashed a torrent of uncoordinated, unmonitored, and naive attempts to help fix a complex situation, not to mention the thousands of unskilled and unprepared volunteers who showed up, hoping to help, yet who lacked the contextual and cultural knowledge to be useful. My first global volunteer experience working in the orphanage in India had been a small example of that very dynamic.

We took note of these important learnings and encouraged people who wanted to volunteer in Nepal to stay home and well out of the way. Luckily, my short stint in Nepal had allowed me just enough time to tap into a small network of relationships made up of guides, travel experts, and nonprofit leaders who would provide a trusted pathway for us to be able to constructively help after the disaster occurred. Our objective was to raise as much funding as we could and to keep it flowing into the hands of these trustworthy people and organizations who were closest to the ground. They would be the best equipped to apply it how and where it was needed most. Making sure contributions traveled directly to transparent, community-led, and organized initiatives had been our mantra before the disaster, and it was more important now than ever.

Within twelve hours of the news, our donor community showed tremendous solidarity, giving generously for a country in deep need. But knowing the extent of the crisis, we needed to expand our reach beyond them. I made my way around Los Angeles, fundraising wherever I could at bookstores, rotary clubs, and community centers.

Anyone who knows me is aware of my intense fear of public speaking; I had struggled with it my whole life. With hands and voice shaking, I would make it through my slideshow of pictures, trying to hold tears back as the memories flooded back. I remember one particular presentation I had been asked to give in conjunction with a man named Carl Werts at Distant Lands, a well-known bookstore in Pasadena. Carl is a dentist and had spent a large part of his free time on volunteer dental missions in underserved areas of the world. He had traveled extensively through Nepal and had collected a fantastic gallery of images. With *Jumping the Picket Fence* recently published, the bookstore thought it would be a great idea to promote the book in conjunction with a fundraising campaign for Nepal. Carl would provide the powerful backdrop of imagery with his stunning gallery of photos.

I was my typical nervous self in the minutes leading up to the presentation. I could feel my heart begin to race as the room filled to capacity, people squeezing into rows of tightly placed folding chairs, some standing in the back. But my nerves melted away and the words flowed freely from my heart as Carl and I made our way through the presentation. Carl described his experience of profound kindness from the Nepalese, and I offered an invitation to do what we each could in the face of the disaster—that our care could be transported. That it mattered.

When we finished, I noticed about a third of the audience was sleeping. Many were local senior citizens who were in the habit of attending whatever was scheduled at the bookstore on the third Wednesday of every month. This hadn't bothered me at all—in fact, the nodding heads had helped ease the stress at the outset. But a good handful had been moved during the hour and a half, and they waited in line afterward to find out how they could help.

One of the people I met was named Larry Meyers. Larry managed the Youssef and Kamel Mawardi Fund, a private foundation that supported a wide range of education initiatives. He, too, had fallen in love with Nepal, and he wanted to learn more details about the exact projects we were funding. We decided to meet the following week at a local breakfast spot in the valley. Over our eggs and coffee, I explained to Larry in more detail where every penny of our funding was going.

We had funded the purchase of brick-making machines in the village of Dadaguan, where I had met the spirited principal Dhorje, so the villagers themselves could compress their own bricks to rebuild their homes, 90 percent of which had been destroyed. At the school TOIT outside of Bhaktapur that I had visited the morning of the earthquake, we had funded food and psychological support for the students and families who had been severely traumatized, not only by the event of that day, but from the endless aftershocks that prolonged their debilitating shock symptoms and prevented them from resuming normal life. And knowing that out-of-school children would fall prey to traffickers, we provided temporary makeshift schools in hard-to-reach mountainous villages.

Larry had listened intently to every word. I was suddenly intrigued to know what had brought him to a life so concentrated on philanthropic work, and to this day, I am so glad I asked. Larry described how, in the late eighties, he was at the top of his game, leading what he felt was his best life. He had a wonderful family life, he enjoyed his work and, as a result of running marathons, he was in the best physical shape of his life. One day while he was driving, he was rear-ended. While the accident hadn't been more than a fender-bender, Larry suffered a ruptured disk. The condition didn't seem too serious at the time, but it later developed into a serious spinal injury, one that could result in paralysis. After undergoing a complex and risky surgery, Larry experienced an amazing full recovery, and slowly, he resumed his active life, marathons and all. But something in him had changed. "I started to ask myself what really mattered. What's the purpose of it all?" he said. Feeling incredibly grateful for his good fortune, he began to fundraise while he ran his marathons, giving back with every mile. The more he did, the more his efforts blossomed.

Two weeks after our meeting, Larry and his daughter Carole provided funds for a grant to build a training center a few hours outside of Kathmandu; they would eventually forge a close partnership with GoPhil. I continued to be in awe of how our little organization was growing, one relationship at a time—what felt painfully slow at times, yet what also revealed such a beautiful unfolding of people coming together, sharing in the responsibility of caring for the world. Meeting people like Larry made the weight of the work feel a little bit lighter.

"Hey Lydia," Larry said as we walked to our cars. "When are you going back to Nepal?" The words swept through me like a tidal wave, and I immediately felt my breakfast turn upside down in my stomach.

"Gosh I don't know—I haven't given that much thought yet."

"Well, my guess is that it is most likely in the cards. But in the meantime, keep up the good work!" he said encouragingly as he waved goodbye.

9

ROOTING AROUND

Open your hands if you want to be held.

—Rumi

AS SUMMER APPROACHED, the mood in the house became increasingly dense—like a heavy, humid blanket. And just when it began to shift and lighten, one of us would pull it back over our shoulders. I slipped deeper into body pain with each passing day. As it became harder to hide, I opened up to John about it, as well as to Linda and Tracey, admitting that there were days I couldn't wade through the agony. But on many days, I hid the anguish, pushing it away with endless hours of work. I was happy to listen to the world's suffering but not ready to acknowledge my own. While I was feeling the pain on a physical level, something was telling me its roots dug way deeper inside of me. I wasn't ready to dig into that patch of ground just yet.

Nick and Emma were busy swimming through their own

storms of emotions. Their music contracts were finalized, signed, and sealed—it was exciting, but there were mixed feelings as the label continued to focus on Emma. Nick's music was ahead of its time, and the executives felt it was the bigger risk in marketing to the mainstream.

We celebrated this momentous occasion with champagne and reluctance, all of us hoping for Nick's day in the sun. Emma wanted that for him probably more than all of us put together; she had never asked to take that from him. Her decision to accept the contract was firmly tied to him—her music was created with him and through him, their voices often intertwined on the tracks. He had worked so hard, for so many years, busking rain or shine at the public market for hours on end, being voted on or kicked off of stages, rehearsing endlessly while being scrutinized for every move, every smile, that wasn't just right for the teenage masses. They would forge ahead together as a team, no matter who was in the lead; she didn't want it otherwise.

Nick got over the initial sting, attempting to see the good in the situation, as he had always done. He would also be making good money as a producer and had a say in building a new state-of-the-art recording studio in West Hollywood. While his own solo career was not on a trajectory yet, he was at least immersed in a world he loved, spending his days learning the deeper technicalities of the production side of the music industry, another angle of the art he would eventually master. They would leave together in the morning, spending entire days in a dark recording studio, returning in the evening, sometimes very late—either ecstatic over what they had created or ready to kill one another. Meetings with the label executives added to the toxicity of the situation, with talks of launching albums and moves to London.

Our collective family blood pressure was running frightfully high. I found Izzy retreating more and more to her walk-in closet. It had become an oasis for her, a world into which she could escape that was distinctly hers. The shelves were covered with precious mementos from China—her adoption photo album and her stuffed animals. Various princess dresses hung over a small handful of special party shoes. John's sister Suzanne had given Izzy her old childhood pair of black patent shoes—oh how she loved to click around in them dressed in her royal costumes. Next to the black ones were the sparkly red pair that Nick had bought her the prior Christmas, just like the ones Dorothy had worn in *The Wizard of Oz*. Shoes made Izzy happy.

But on the floor were hundreds of her most treasured items on earth—her books. This is where she found her greatest safety and peace. And while I worried about the length of time she spent reading in her closet, it was better than her facing the seriousness of the rest of the house. She had had enough serious in her life; she didn't need more.

It was high time for us to break the routine—to find laughter and fun again—to play. I don't remember who made the suggestion to go to Costa Rica, but we all jumped on the idea. We already had a long love affair with the country, beginning even before the kids had been born. Besides visiting my family in Europe a couple of times in our teens, our three weeks in Costa Rica had been the first big trip John and I had taken, our first true adventure as a couple. A few years later when it had become clear that more typical life choices were not going to be part of our story, we returned as a family. I had been experiencing a midlife crisis, questioning the path to "success" we were on as young executive search consultants in Orlando. Nick and Ems had made their entry into our world, and I was desperately torn between the career I was building and the emerging yet daunting task of being a mother. I also felt a strange pull inside my soul that was begging me to consider a different path altogether.

Costa Rica represented our first refuge as a family, a safe place to begin to unpack what wasn't working for us as a couple and to reexamine where we were headed. After six weeks in the nest of the Pacific rainforest, where the noise of life lowered itself to a level where we could hear ourselves once again, we gained enough clarity to take some active steps into building a life on our own terms. We scraped together every penny we had, borrowing from our savings, and bought a house in Manuel Antonio on the Pacific Coast, renting it to tourists by the week as an income-producing property. We returned often to soak up the oxygen and green that felt so good, so grounding, and to absorb the sensation of being free, away from the grips of US life and what it was feeding us, a cycle we knew we needed to break.

It had been fun, new terrain for us—a foreign place to explore and a new business to develop. We had no idea at the time that our future family business would involve building a luxury villa rental brand abroad. The combination of stillness, earthiness, and independence that we experienced in Costa Rica gave us a hunger for more of it. One day, we packed our bags, sold the house and car in Orlando, and moved to the south of France. We never looked back.

Returning to Costa Rica for a vacation was tempting, yet it was also a place we knew well. Why not venture out and try something new? But I had traveled so much in the past years that I simply didn't have the motivation it took to research someplace different. I desperately needed to get my footing and energy back. I was floundering, still in a fog, going through the normal daily functions, yet semi-unhinged. *We could plant ourselves in Manuel Antonio, the kids knew their way around, and I could see my dear friend Adrienne. I could take some yoga classes and run my usual route up the big hill from the beach near the National Park. I'm sure ten days in Manuel will turn this problem around—I just need a bit of R&R, that's all.*

"Yessssss," Emma screeched. "Let's do it. That's exactly what we all need—a bit of jungle air." Emma was always particularly happy there. As a child, she loved observing the wildlife that roamed freely, the iguanas, monkeys, and sloths—there was so much to take in during a day.

The moment our feet hit the ground, I felt us all take a collective breath. Tired from taking the red-eye into San Jose, nobody said much on the windy, three-hour drive over the mountains and down the coast, past Playa Herradura and Jaco Beach. When the kids were little, one of them invariably got carsick on the first leg, and by the time we reached our house, sweaty and hungry, we felt we had earned our way to the sanctuary—and to the local bar for a cold margarita.

But I knew my people well enough that the silence in the car meant we had already begun to wrap ourselves up in a place of comfort and security that we had always found in Costa Rica, one that we would later carry with us wherever we went on the road.

We had sold our house that we had owned years before in Manuel Antonio, so we settled into a hotel at the top of the hill. We could walk down to a quiet private beach or take the main road down to a public one at the entrance of the National Park. But the best part about our location was that it was directly across the street from Café Milagro and El Patio—the café and restaurant that Adrienne and her business partner, Lance, owned.

After unpacking, I made my way outside and across the street to see her. I knocked on her office door, she opened it, and I fell into her arms—soaking in the familiar smell of her thick, curly hair. "Oh Lyd, it's so great to see you," she said, pulling back to take a good look at me. I could tell she was scanning my face, looking for my true state. Ade was one of those friends it was impossible to hide anything from.

It didn't take long for the heaping tears to flow. I unloaded it all, my new self that didn't seem right, my aches and pains, the fears over the kids and their futures, my heart that was endlessly wrapped up and entangled in GoPhil's work with people who I felt had real problems to deal with. "I've lost my grip, Adrienne. I don't have it all together anymore. I'm not that strong and courageous woman in *Jumping the Picket Fence*. I don't know who I am or where I am going. I just hurt all over, in every way." I laid the whole mixed-up mess safely on her plate without taking a breath. True to form, Ade just listened patiently, accepting it, taking it all in. After I was done, I looked up. She said one thing: "You need to see Evelina. I'll make the appointment."

John and I had known Evelina from our earlier days when we had owned a house there. Evelina was from Italy, and at that time, she was mainly doing massage therapy for tourists alongside making her own natural body products. She discovered Pilates, which she credits with helping her to recover completely from a herniated disk in her neck. Over the years, Evelina had deeply committed herself to expanding her field of study. Her practice led her to the realization that what was going on inside of her had meaning outside of her, and vice versa. She learned to embrace her own fragility, and in return it became her strength. Over time, she had become a gifted holistic energy healer.

"What brings you in?" she asked nonchalantly, as if no years had passed since my last appointment.

"Well, I have this pain going down my right arm and into my thumb—which is now completely numb. And I'm kind of tender all over, and I am very lethargic," I added. Wanting to keep things simple, I didn't tell her about the agonizing body pain that was slowly consuming me whole.

"How long has this been going on?"

"Since about April—I was in Nepal while there was an earthquake."

"Hmm. Tell me what went through your mind the minute it happened," she asked.

I hadn't been expecting to be thrown back to that day right then and there. I took a big breath and looked up to the corner of the room, willing myself not to get sucked into the vortex of emotions. "The children—and John," I said. "They flashed through my mind. I thought I was going to die. That I would never see them again."

Evelina then reminded me of the last time I had seen her,

several years prior. In that session, she was experimenting with an emerging technique called Diagnostic Internal Energy. After placing small slides on my body and asking questions about major events in my life, she was able to see where blockages were located. "You have safety issues—root chakra imbalances," she had said. I had done a fair amount of energy work, so I knew the significance of the root chakra, often referred to as our survival center. It's the chakra of stability, security, and our basic needs. "These issues extend to your children as your need to protect now extends to them. Your moves around the world have been a wonderful experience and discovery, but there is also an element of fleeing as well, of running away."

Maybe the blockages she had found back then still applied now. We had been moving around as a family for the past fifteen years. Our homes in both Costa Rica and Provence had become businesses that required us to move in and out of their spaces. We had traveled a lot, and it was incredibly enriching, especially as we channeled our efforts into building GoPhil. But we had also lived a rather untethered lifestyle, and this had been difficult on each of us at different times. I felt that, despite loving the freedom, in some way I had been rooting around, trying to find a home, but never really finding it. I had almost given up on the idea, thinking that maybe we just weren't meant to have one, that our home was found in simply being together as a family. This concept of fleeing had not resonated at all before, but now, in the context of the earthquake, it took some form. Leaving Nepal had felt like escaping, like running away from a situation that was unsafe, but it also felt like I was abandoning something. And in a deep, dark corner of my soul, I knew it wasn't the only time I had tried to run from something I couldn't handle, something terribly unsafe.

Evelina and I chatted for over an hour. She asked me more about the day of the earthquake and about how my body was feeling. There was no massage, no fancy energy work or essential oils. She didn't touch me. She just listened and scanned in a profoundly intuitive way.

"So what do I need to do—you know, for this stupid thumb-numbing thing to go away?" I asked, wondering what sort of new treatments she might suggest. I looked at the cool straps they were using for upside down yoga classes. "I have a full ten days here, Evelina. Time enough for several sessions, daily classes even."

"No," she said. "You are to do nothing. No treatments, no yoga, no running—none of that. That pain in your arm comes from believing that you would no longer hold your children— from a subconscious fear you could no longer protect them. Eat whatever you want, get up early or sleep late. Listen to your body's rhythms—honor them," Evelina said. "Sleep, eat, walk. Nurture yourself. You need to heal. It is going to take some time." And she sent me on my way.

I chewed on Evelina's words over and over as I walked back to the hotel under the hot midday sun. I might have been stomping just a little bit. The session was not what I had been expecting. It was uncomfortable. I wanted to take active steps in getting back to normal. I wanted to *DO* something and get on with life. *Nurture myself? What did that look like? I know how to care for John, my children, the dog; I know how to care for the programs we worked alongside at GoPhil. But myself?*

And then I remembered she used the word "heal." I knew Evelina enough to know that she wasn't using the word lightly. She was a wise soul, and she had said just enough for me to want to know more. Explaining it to me would be undermining the essence of what I needed to understand. I needed to discover it. For the moment, the word would hang suspended in the air, in my mind, without much to hinge itself on.

10

A NEW REALM
OPENING

THE DAYS SLIPPED AWAY, the kids and John having a ball doing what we normally did in Manuel Antonio—playing at the beach and eating and hanging with Ade at Café Milagro—breakfast, lunch, and sometimes dinner. We sat silently under the afternoon rains and watched the monkeys and sloths play in the jungle, and I started my masterclass in doing nothing. The more I thought about it, the more intrigued I became with letting go, of releasing this incessant, perpetual habit of executing something at all times. I was curious about what I might discover on this other side of *doing*.

Granted, somewhere in my mind, I had also convinced myself that this examination would only last in earnest for the duration of the trip. Real life would be waiting for me afterward, and whatever I figured out during this time away would help me going forward, I thought. Looking back, I treated these first steps like an exercise of sorts, or a diet—like an optional healthy thing to do to feel better. What I didn't understand fully was that a powerful shift, a massive transformation, was underway, and I wasn't at all in control of it. I could try as I might to put off the work I needed to do—I could pick it up and put it down—but time would tell that I wouldn't be allowed to get very far until I had to face it again. We humans are pretty smart, but we are also totally delusional when it comes to thinking we are in control.

One day the kids and John packed up our four-wheel-drive rental car, dirty with sand and wet towels from days at the beach, and went out with Ade to her property, which had a fantastic water-fall to jump off of. Not feeling in the mood to fling my physical self off a cliff, I stayed back. I considered all of the nothing I could do and decided on a walk down the quiet private path that led from the top of our road where we were staying to a secluded beach.

I was wearing flips-flops and it was a little steep, so I watched my footing carefully as I went. At some point along the way, I looked to my right on the side of the trail and noticed an incredibly large root that led to an even larger trunk of a tree. *Holy shit, this thing is larger than life.* Looking up toward the jungle canopy, I was able to get a better perspective on its girth, which was unlike anything I had ever seen before. At the age of forty-five, I would think that I would have experienced seeing a large tree before, but this was on another dimension. It made the pine trees in my backyard look like saplings. Taking slow and deliberate steps, I approached this magnificent tree, stopping about a foot away to get a better look.

We stood facing each other, looking at one another—with her big, strong trunk, long and lean arms, and muscular roots—and me, a tiny fraction of her height with little feet, plastic flip-flops, and a numb thumb. In a strange sense, I felt as if I was being introduced to someone. I became distinctly aware that I was being asked to greet it—greet *her*, somehow. In that moment, I was sure, shit sure even, that this living being was communicating with me. I just stood there, speechless and paralyzed, trying to hear what she was saying.

For several minutes, I did nothing but soak in the warm bath of energy that seemed to be spreading from her into my body, pulling me further into her space. Then I began to notice the most beautiful bright green moss that covered her trunk, and I was struck with a sudden overwhelming urge to reach out and touch it. I took a few steps and held out my fingers to feel her bright softness, a living carpet that spread up her tall trunk as far as I could see. Before I knew it, my arms were outstretched as I embraced her fully, letting the side of my face sit gently against her. My arms clutched the only thing that felt right at that moment, the only thing that had felt right for so many weeks—or had it been longer, had it been a lot, lot longer? Time stopped as I became enveloped into the belly of something so loving, so comfortable, so safe.

Her physical presence was nothing short of tremendous, yet I didn't feel intimidated in the least, or even small. I felt connected, like she was a part of me and I a part of her. I wondered whether this was her—Mother Earth. But it seemed bigger and broader than just the earth. It seemed to encompass everything. *Was this the Oneness I had heard about but had yet to truly feel?* Whatever it was, it was nothing short of magnificent, and I felt a surge of energy followed by the most incredible sense of gratitude. When I finally felt ready to step back, I took a big, deep breath.

"Wow. Thank you. For whatever that was. Thank you."

As I backed up and carried on down the path, I asked myself—
What the hell just happened? I think I even looked back over my
shoulder to make sure nobody had witnessed the strangeness of
what had just transpired. I made it to the beach but didn't stay
long. I trudged back up to the hotel in a bit of a daze, smiling to
the tree as I passed. I then thought about all that had happened
in just a few short months. I felt I was being gently introduced to
a new way of interpreting the world around me, of listening to it.
And it had seemed like an offering, a gift that was precisely what
I needed, right at that moment. My old tools that previously had
worked well in life—being industrious, determined and driven—
didn't suffice anymore.

In these early months, it would be too soon to understand
that my trying to solve or fix things that seemed wrong with the
world, or with myself, had run its course. It was as though the
earthquake had blown all that apart, expanding the dimension of
what had been a limited view of all there was to experience. All of
a sudden, I saw so much more. Another realm of seeing and feeling
was emerging, and it seemed to be based on an exchange or flow of
energy, from places I had never felt it coming from before. Some
greater force was reaching out to me, and I felt like I was being
asked to receive it.

I was sad that our time in Costa Rica was coming to an end.
The trip had offered me more than I had expected, but one more
blessing was in store.

"Lyd—meet Travis Day; Travis, meet Lyd. I know you'll love
each other, so have at it," Ade chuckled as she marched into the back

kitchen of the café. We ordered coffee and set about to get to know one another. Travis was originally from the East Coast, Boston and Maine, and had moved to Costa Rica the year prior. He was living and working at an organic farm and hotel in the central part of the country, helping out with their website, graphic design, and social media. I immediately sensed a warmth to Travis, and the next hour easily flew by as we chatted about each other's lives.

"I was at a turning point in my life when I left the US," Travis explained. "I was running a company that I had built with a friend of mine. It was called Equifit, and offered an innovative line of equipment and clothing for horses. Over the years, it became a hit in the high-end equestrian world, and we were at the height of pretty significant success. But something was off, and I just knew in my heart that it wasn't the path for me. One night I just decided that was it—I wanted a life built around other things, more meaningful things. So I sold it all and left."

I had a distinct feeling that this man was very special—something was different about him. I couldn't quite put my finger on it at the time, but I knew he walked with a unique kind of powerful grace, a kindness coupled with deep principle—the kind of man the world could use a lot more of. We spoke at length about GoPhil, about its mission to offer greater voice to people and programs who were taking brave action in the face of inequities. I described our roles on the team and how we each wore a gazillion hats. "I do all things relating to donor communications, website, blog, messaging, marketing, PR ... that kind of thing. I've just put together our next three-year communication and marketing plan. Would you consider having a look? Just for another set of eyes?" I asked boldly.

Travis pulled his computer over and was already scanning our website. "Sure. Send it over; let me take a look. I'll get back to you with some feedback."

Travis and I met again a day or so later at the café. He was full of thoughts and ideas and didn't hesitate in being direct about what was lacking. "For starters, Lydia, where is your logo? You need a symbol that represents the work you do in bringing people together to share in the work, a logo that is recognizable," he stated matter-of-factly.

And just as each and every team member at GoPhil over the years had seemed to magically appear at just the right time, with just the right skills, Travis didn't delay in getting to work. He helped with our logo, which ended up being a circle of interconnected people joined by their hands and feet spinning from a single point in the center. It was a perfect reflection of our mission. This was just the beginning, a grain of sand on what would later be a beautiful seashore of love and care this man would bring into the GoPhil fold. The fact that he walked into my life right at the moment when I wasn't sure from where I would continue to draw my energy reinforced a growing knowing that silent, mystical maneuvers were happening underneath all that was going on.

Our little family respite in Manuel Antonio came to an end—it felt far too short, but the beginnings of something new had developed during our time there, and the days had been more beneficial than I ever could have imagined. I felt I had taken my first breath in a long time. Evelina's wise words, the big tree, and the beginnings of nothingness were baby steps in a thousand-step journey toward looking at my place and purpose in a different way. For starters, I was being forced to acknowledge and honor myself, my own health and presence, in that equation. It was also a hint that healing might be linked to the energy and wisdom inherent in the natural world, to the earth, and that it offered a source for us all. And it was all there at our feet.

The kids needed to return to LA early, as they were due to start recording Emma's album. John, Izzy, and I were to carry on to Guatemala where some GoPhil work awaited. I was sad to see Nick and Emma leave. A van collected them at 4 a.m. one morning for the three-hour drive to San Jose, where they would catch their onward flight. But it also felt right. We had taken a moment to stop and play. And in doing so, we had returned to a baseline that felt good. *Play, grace, and clarity* were slowly revealing themselves to me.

11

HARMONY

HER VOICE RATTLED AS SHE SPOKE, rapid-fire Spanish tumbled from her mouth, her eyes locked onto mine, never once stopping to blink. I picked up on some of the words, attempting to string together the story that Maria Elena was describing with such heartfelt passion. The lines in her face bore the evidence of pain that seemed to come from deep down into the core of her being. But she also carried a warrior type of love as she spoke of the Mayan communities she served out of her health clinic in the highlands of San Andrés Itzapa in Guatemala. It was clear to me from that first encounter that Maria Elena was among one of the great messengers of our time; someone who was put on this earth to show us—with her own blood, sweat, and tears—what needed to be done.

The GoPhil team had been talking about broadening our wing-span for years, and the timing was right to begin the long process of scouting and vetting new partnerships. Guatemala had been on the shortlist, and conveniently, it was only a hop-skip from Costa Rica. I had actually traveled down there years prior for a potential collaboration with Habitat for Humanity—they were considering private trips for donors who couldn't manage the intense physical nature of their house builds. They hoped GoPhilanthropic Travel, with its experience in managing the complexities of donor journeys, could manage the trips for them. But even after many months of massaging the idea, meeting the Habitat teams in both Guatemala and in their home office in Atlanta, the proposal got stuck in administrative red tape and never went any further. I had been terribly disappointed at the time, wanting very much to understand how to help what appeared to me to be a desperately poor country. But looking back, I am now relieved that we hadn't ventured into the region in the wake of such a large charitable organization. Our smaller and simpler structure allowed us to take our own careful steps in entering new areas, patiently following the lead of the small programs we discovered were doing the work few others would undertake. We didn't drive the agendas of their initiatives or the timelines of their projects. We just came with the willingness to help them with their most pressing needs—funding-wise or operationally. Our goals had always been rooted in developing strength in their own self-reliance, as opposed to dependence on donors; We wanted nothing more than to see them spread their wings even further.

At times we felt as though our contributions were just a drop in the big bucket of need, and they were—and still are—but only if you base the comparison on financial terms. Our gentler pace allows us a window into how communities are addressing the root causes of their own problems, in their own ways. Our partner programs are showing us the importance of driving change from within, as opposed to just leaning on help from the outside. They might be deemed poor by the world at large, as I had perceived Guatemala to be years prior, yet this is not the lens from which our partners view themselves. They are focused on the resources they do have, even if they are not immediately recognized by outsiders on the surface. They are not short on the vigor or drive needed to walk the long journey to gain just and equal access to health services, education, and human rights, and they are not lacking in wisdom and knowledge derived from their long and rich heritages.

The Maya, like so many other areas made up of large numbers of indigenous communities, have a long history of exploitation and discrimination in their own homeland—an ugly legacy left by colonialism. Guatemala's overall population is about 60 percent Mayan; in more rural areas, over 98 percent of the population identifies as indigenous. Yet they are still the underprivileged majority of Guatemala's population. Although Guatemala is the largest economy in Central America, it trails its neighboring countries in almost all social and economic aspects. Its human development index, a composite measure of life expectancy, income, and education, is the lowest of any other country in the region.

In the early 1960s, a civil war broke out between the government and indigenous groups who no longer accepted the inequalities that existed in economic and political life. In the 1970s, the Maya began participating in protests against the repressive government, demanding greater equality and inclusion of the Mayan language and culture. In 1980, the Guatemalan army instituted

"Operation Sophia," horrific acts of genocide specifically targeting the Mayan population, who were believed to be supporting the guerrilla movement.

Over the next three years, the army destroyed over six hundred villages, killing an estimated two hundred thousand people and displacing an additional 1.5 million. More than 150,000 were driven to seek refuge in Mexico. Forced disappearance policies included secretly arresting or abducting people, who were often killed and buried in unmarked graves. The government instituted a scorched earth policy, destroying and burning buildings and crops, slaughtering livestock, fouling water supplies, and violating sacred places and cultural symbols. The US government often supported the repressive regimes as part of its anti-Communist policies during the Cold War.

The details of Maria Elena's story would unfold later that day and slowly over the years we have spent as partners. Julio, one of the four sons who helps her run the health clinic, took me to a quiet spot in the kitchen area on that first meeting and explained the harrowing yet powerful history behind the health center. Maria had spent years working as a nurse, serving disadvantaged Mayan communities alongside her brother who was a doctor, whom she loved dearly.

During the civil war, many health care professionals, including Maria Elena's brother, were targeted and brutally killed. Devastated, yet wanting to carry on the legacy of her brother's commitment to providing health services to marginalized Mayan communities, the tragedy became the catalyst for Maria Elena to open up the center. ASSADE, as it is called, now treated over ten thousand patients a year on a shoestring annual budget of fifty thousand dollars.

"But Lydia, there is a very important purpose behind our approach to medicine and healing," Julio explained. "In order to build a successful health care model here in Guatemala, it is necessary to include traditional indigenous medicine. This involves a respectful relationship to take into consideration. It has to do with the balance between nature, justice, equality, humanism, and love."

Central to Mayan medicine, which is holistic in nature, rests the belief in "ch'ulel," a life force that exists in each of us and in all of the physical world around us. The body and soul, which are metaphors for the natural and spiritual realms, are interwoven and interconnected. Ch'ulel life force can be found in everything from our bodies to plants, animals, buildings, and mountains. If one area is ill or lacks a life force, it will affect other areas, compromising the whole system. Our universe, they believe, is ruled by the same principle that everything is interconnected. Healing is about restoring the inherent balance and harmony of all things—no single component being more important than another.

I listened intently, soaking in his stories. I didn't entirely understand what he was saying, but what he was sharing was resonating with me beyond his words. We walked around the clinic while Julio explained the various services they provided, which ranged from treating common yet preventable gastrointestinal and respiratory problems, to women's reproductive issues—Mayan communities faced an unusually high rate of ovarian cancer. He walked me up a narrow, winding staircase and opened a door to a room that appeared to be used as storage. "You see these two dental chairs, Lydia?" I scanned the room and found them, dusty and neglected.

"They were a donation but they need to be repaired. It is our dream to offer oral health care here—but we are a long way. We will need a dentist, of course," he said with a little chuckle.

At the end of my tour, I pointed to a catchment tank that I assumed held water. It seemed small to me. "Do you have sufficient clean water?" I asked, concerned. "We only have running water for two hours a day, but we make do," he said as he led me to the next room.

Later, when ASSADE submitted their grant application to GoPhil, we had expected a focus on expanding their access to water. We were surprised it was not—a clear example of how an outside perspective couldn't understand the inside context that drove their priorities. They had found a way to adequately conserve water and to do it within two hours. Maybe we couldn't comprehend this so easily since we have access to water at all times—and are incredibly wasteful with it as a result. Their priority was oral health care, which was virtually nonexistent in the region yet was such a critical element to well-being. They wanted to fix their dental chair and hire a dentist.

For the following years, we would guide many small groups to the ASSADE clinic, and Julio, in his soft-spoken but powerful manner, would share the important, fundamental interplay of nature, equality, and love that formed the basis of their work at their clinic. Maria Elena would stand firmly in the background, smiling, exuding her strength, determination, and fierce compassion. Julio would then take us to the nearby traditional Mayan spiritual site of San Simón, where we could observe shamans tending to spiritual fires and conducting religious ceremonies for people, many of whom were seeking relief from health issues. ASSADE recognized these traditions as an integral part of its health care program.

I had been to many rural clinics in different places around the world, and I had never heard health care described in the way Maria Elena's family described it at ASSADE. It would take time to ingest the scope of their beliefs, a beautiful blend of traditional and Western medicine. We had always seen our work as helping people fight for their right to health care or education. These rights were achieved— people acquired them, as if there were tangible things to take back, like chips on a board. But if you looked at this through this ancient Mayan lens, it wasn't about getting one's fair share of a pie. It was about restoring and rebalancing—redistributing a flow, an endless abundance of what was meant to be there in the first place. I realized that when Julio had described health, the words justice and equality were embedded in between nature, humanism, and love, as if they naturally occurred when that harmony was in place.

I thought about this a lot over that first week as we acclimated ourselves to Antigua, walking the cobblestone streets of the small colonial city surrounded by volcanos. It had become a tourist haven, with trendy boutiques, chocolate shops, and wine bars, yet had also maintained a serenity not always found in the travel hotspots. As night descended, the restaurants would empty before ten, the streets becoming quiet, and only the soft rumble of the odd car driving over stony roads could be heard alongside the faint trickle of fountains.

Many of the city's monuments had been destroyed by earth-quakes, which had plagued the region for hundreds of years. Ancient cathedrals stood proudly, lacking rooftops; enormous chunks of arches and pillars remained on the ground like unfinished puzzles. *Piles of stones*, I thought. *I can't quite seem to get away from them.*

One morning we stumbled on San Francisco Church, Iglesia de San Francisco, a stunning colonial structure. Along the right side of the church were the ruins of a sanctuary that at one time was home to over a hundred Franciscan friars. While the church itself was intact, much of the sanctuary had been destroyed in earthquakes. The three of us wandered through the winding pathways of the ancient ruins, through its crumbled walls with crawling bougainvillea and ivy. Birds flew in and out of the roofless structures, and the trees sang as they swayed. While Izzy and John continued to wind their way through the old, rounded cave-like rooms where prayers and meals were served, I stopped, not wanting to go any further. Taking deep breaths, I soaked in the peacefulness of the site, marveling at the beauty that had remained after such destruction.

On the side of the sanctuary was a small museum devoted to a missionary known as Hermano Pedro. He had arrived in Antigua in the 1600s on the heels of an earthquake. Hungry and destitute, he had joined the bread lines, but he also walked the streets at night ringing a bell, sharing what bread he had and tending to the sick. Hermano Pedro spent the rest of his life devoted to caring for the ill and destitute. Hundreds of years after his death, he would become a saint. His tomb had become a pilgrimage site where people come to pray for miracles.

I stood there, completely amazed that the walls of the museum were adorned with thousands and thousands of tokens of gratitude—for the blessings and miracles people believed had come from prayers made to Hermano Pedro. You couldn't help but feel consumed with the presence of grace and gratitude while walking through those halls.

On the one hand, I was overwhelmed with what I had learned of Guatemala's tragic and traumatic past. I saw so much evidence of trauma, from its destroyed buildings to such a terribly unjust system that prevented indigenous peoples from being able to thrive. In the moment, I felt sucked into a vortex, continuously surrounded by so much that needed fixing. The broken dentist chair stuck out in my mind, a simple symbol of all that was undone.

Was the task to put it all back together, or was it to accept things as they were? Maybe it was neither. I just didn't know. All I could do in the face of that question, as the sun made its way down, was to find peace in the moment amongst the ruins and walls of thanks and gratitude. I took a mental picture of the tranquility found on those grounds, knowing I could return there in my mind whenever I needed. Maybe what we were being called to do was less about putting things back together and more about the healing and harmony Julio had described so eloquently.

Later that week, it was time for Izzy to travel bravely, as an unaccompanied minor, to see my Mum and her husband, Magnus, in Toronto, then to John's parents in Saratoga Springs. Like Nick and Emma, she would be asked to take long journeys, oftentimes on her own, to see her family who lived across many countries.

I sat with her at the airport, doing what I could to calm her nerves before separating for two weeks. She picked at the colored sprinkles on the donut I had bought her to lighten the mood. "You'll be great, Iz. You've got so many people who love you and want to spend time with you. Time with grandparents is special—and they are going to spoil you rotten," I tempted. She had been asked to be brave so many times in her life—this was just one time more. She admitted to not liking the experience because she had never flown from Guatemala before. "I am scared," she said, her voice starting to quiver.

"Baby, our lives are going to be about not knowing. It's going to be a whole series of not-knowings and not-having-done-befores. Let's just dig down and find the knowing that things will be fine—that they will, in fact, be great," I said, squeezing her hand. She cried a little, then adjusted her new little embroidered Guatemalan bag that held a book and a journal, arranging it tightly around her shoulder.

Who was I to tell a girl who had lost so much in her young life that things would be fine? Did I have that right? Did I even believe it myself?

The airline attendant approached us, and we hugged goodbye. I watched as she walked away, turning back only once to make sure I was still there. I could tell she was still teary but knew from her step that she trusted she would be fine. Tears are OK, my sweetheart, as long as there is trust. Yes—I did believe it. We can face the unknown if we trust that a big and beautiful story is waiting for us on the other side of that fear.

I returned to Antigua and joined John, who was waiting at the Hotel Rafael, the small, serene seven-bedroom hotel where we had been staying. I climbed into the soft bed, John pouring me a glass of red wine—he knew that I, too, was teary at any separation involving the kids.

"I swear, the whole having-children thing is all about letting them go. From the minute you give birth, you begin the process of letting go. How can you protect and let go at the same time? It's impossible," I said, tucking myself into his arms. I could feel the subtle movement of life was asking me to take the same advice I had given to Izzy. I had to trust that the world would treat them with care. I could only give them so much protection before it got in the way of them discovering their own strengths. I gazed up at the big painting above the bed, where a near-life-size image of Archangel Raphael—said to be responsible for healing—hung over our heads.

We spent the remaining time visiting with other small NGOs, battling challenges resulting from indigenous discrimination. I was thrilled to have reconnected with a program in Central Maya that offered services to people with disabilities around Lake Atitlan. I had met the founder, Leticia, years back when we were considering the partnership with Habitat for Humanity. After meeting her and experiencing the beauty and importance of what she was providing with such little resources, I dreamed of GoPhil being in a position to help her. At the time we were not, and I had carried my memories of her since. Seven years later, we sat facing each other—both of us beaming at the reconnection, about its possibilities.

On our last evening, John and I sat on the terrace of a local restaurant overlooking the plumes spouting from the volcano. I thought about the depth of what was present in Guatemala—a region that I, along with the greater world at large, had labeled sick and poor, yet had so much to teach us.

What steps did we need to take to all heal, to restore the health that the world so desperately needed? Perhaps it was time to question whether the answers, whether our medicine, was "out there." I was beginning to have an inkling that this journey toward restoration, toward harmony, needed to begin inside each of us. Maybe we already possessed what we needed to make things the way they were meant to be; we just needed to return to it. Either way, I promised myself to be completely open to whatever it took to understand what the earth and sky were trying to say. Back at the hotel, feeling small and confused and a little scared, I looked up at Raphael one last time. *All right then, you have my full attention. What next?*

On the way home from the Los Angeles airport, I wondered in what state I would find the house—leaving two teenagers for ten days had been a bit of a risk. Then I remembered my vegetable strip on the side of the house, which I hadn't been present to tend to. My heart sank a little, but I caught it in free-fall—*You can't do everything, Lydia, the break was important. You aren't responsible for everything.*

Nick and Emma were beaming when we walked into the house. "How was Guatemala, Ma?" Emma asked, giving me a big hug. "It was really great," I said as I took a quick glance around. The house was in relative disarray, though there seemed to be some mild attempts at tidying. I noticed the counters were clear yet covered in crumbs and spots of olive oil. But just then I noticed something else, something more important than the crumbs, and my heart exploded. There on my counter was the most massive, beautiful zucchini.

"Oh Mom—we took care of your vegetables! We watered them every day and look what I found," Emma screeched, pointing to the zucchini with excitement. "Isn't it great? We knew you would be so happy."

In that moment, it was clear that it wasn't just me that had given birth to that gorgeous zucchini, but a whole set of energies in motion—my desire to make it happen, a loving husband who tended the soil, and the kids who had watched over the garden while I was gone. Mother Nature had done most of the work, of course, but we had added belief and some care, and it had turned out all right. Together, we could help each other in bringing our simple gifts to dry, cracked, forgotten strips of earth.

I was thrilled. A few days later, we discovered some tomatoes had emerged, and for the next few weeks, we ate them along with Swiss chard and more large zucchinis. I called my sister in the UK. "Helene, it has been confirmed. I am officially not an idiot."

12

UNBECOMING

*The challenges of life are less about what we should
do and more about what we are called to be.*

—Andrew Harvey

"MOM, DO YOU WANT TO GO ON A RUN to Cathedral
Rock?" Emma yelled from the end of the hallway. The trail to the
Cathedral point in our nearby Topanga State Park was a favorite
of mine. It was a tough and oftentimes very hot experience to get
there, but always worth it. On a clear day, you could see the coast-
line on one side all the way down to Venice Beach, as well as the
mountains near Big Bear.

Normally I would go, even if I didn't really want to or had other
things to do. If someone in the family asked me to do anything, I
would pretty much do it. But during this period of fragility and
self-discovery, something had changed.

"Absolutely not," I yelled back without hesitation.

"Wait what?" Emma responded as she pushed open the door to my bedroom where I was working, pulling her leg into her running pants as she went.

"What do you mean?"

"I mean NO. I don't want to go."

"But why—when do you ever not want to go to Cathedral Rock?"

"Actually, way more often than you know, but I do it anyway—I'm a mother."

"Yeah but *why*—why do you go if you don't want to? That's dumb," she said matter-of-factly, as if it had never ever crossed her mind to do something she didn't want to do.

And funnily enough, it probably hadn't. Raising Emma had been a lesson in patience and choosing battles. From the earliest age, I attempted to get her to do the most basic of things—wear a dress, eat something new, or return a smile to a stranger walking by who had greeted us kindly. I think "no" had been her first word, and I had found it incredibly maddening—yet deep down I had tremendous respect for a child who knew her boundaries.

I decided when she was seven that in order to keep the peace, and my sanity, I would have to choose my battles with Emma selectively, picking the ones that were the most morally important and then driving them home without wavering. Brushing her hair or having a clean room never quite made the cut. The system had worked like a charm, but I also had to accept not getting my way most of the time. For a year, the only shoes she wore were a pair of Nick's cowboy boots.

Emma was OK with my no on that day—in fact, I might

have even earned a little respect. But it wasn't the only place I was expressing my real needs. I was also saying no to doing the dishes, cooking favorite meals, to sex—no to anything I didn't want or that felt like an obligation. And it felt more than good. It felt powerful and necessary.

It was during this time that I realized my lifelong habit of running was something I wanted less of. Lacing up those shoes fell somewhere between a duty and a punishment. I had been running since I was fifteen, and I remember my first long jogging outings like they were yesterday—wearing my old blue track pants and blaring Bruce Springsteen on my Walkman, I would run down the long country roads that stretched past the pristine suburbs of Rochester, New York, losing myself in the music and endless rows of corn fields, escaping the loneliness that I was sure would consume me whole.

My parents had divorced and my mother had moved back to Canada, where my sister and I had been born, to start a life with an old family friend. My father was also beginning a new chapter, with a much younger wife. I would come to love these partners much later, grateful for the joy they each brought my parents, but at that moment, I was a hurt and confused teenager and far from accepting them. To add to an already complicated time, John, whom I had fallen madly in love with as a sophomore in high school, had left for college, as had my sister, Helene. Life as I knew it had become a deep ache.

Running wasn't a euphoric evasion from all of this—I actually found it hard and unpleasant. But that was why it worked. One pain replaced the other. But I could control the pain from running, when I brought it on and when I turned it off. I also stopped eating—just one more attempt to deny the losses I was failing to understand. The overall strategy, despite being counterintuitive as well as counterproductive, was to silence one hurt with another. If you deny your needs, you can pretend you never required anything in the first place. In a sense, you become invisible—to yourself.

Thankfully, running became the enjoyable, healthy outlet it should be later in my life, and I started eating again, reluctantly. But the habit of ignoring and denying my own basic needs, of turning my back on a body that wanted to be listened to and nurtured, had perhaps worked its way into my being. Enter motherhood with three children, where by nature I put their needs before my own, combined with a work life that involved supporting people who were fighting for basic rights, and you have the makings of a martyr—aka a *sufferer*.

Previously, if you asked me what I wanted for my birthday or for Christmas, I might have told you nothing—I don't need a thing. I distinctly remember that happening one Christmas. I had been so adamant in professing my need for nothing that the kids and John actually thought that would make me happy.

Now, as a new me was emerging, I found myself rattling off long lists of items that I wanted for myself—cozy scarves, various books, large candles. "Guys, I really want that blue sweater I saw in the boutique last week, the one with the floppy turtleneck. And that pair of really nice soft leather Italian boots!" I added.

It wasn't as if these changes were happening consciously; it was as if they were unfolding all on their own accord. Perhaps not coincidentally, though, I had finally learned to meditate, something

John and I had both been talking about for a long time. With all that had happened in the past year, it seemed like a good moment to embrace it. It was also incredibly trendy, especially in LA, and I wanted to know for myself what all of the fuss was about. For all these reasons, and a few more, meditation was calling, and I was ready. John might have seemed an unlikely character to jump into it—he could come across as the logical, driven, independent entrepreneur type. But he also had a child-like openness and curiosity, a willingness for things unknown. "Yeah—bring it on," he had said after I suggested we take the course.

This common curiosity was probably why we made a good match—we didn't avoid what we hadn't tried. Our moves around the world and steps we had taken to start projects in which we had no backgrounds were evidence that fear over the unknown had not played much of a role in our lives. It had, though, made for a fair amount of fumbling and tumbling along the way. I distinctly remember the moment after we had moved to Costa Rica to start a catamaran tour boat business when we realized we had bitten off more than we could chew. After four months, we packed up and moved back to Provence with our tails between our legs. But the courage to try had also been the foundation for everything else that had worked out.

We signed up for a Transcendental Meditation class, more commonly referred to as TM. Enough was out there in the general body of knowledge surrounding meditation to know that it was a simple yet powerful practice. I longed for anything at that moment that could help dull the noise of my disoriented state. The course was pricey, but people raved about how easy it was to learn—and that's what I was seeking, a beeline to Zen. The struggle so many people had encountered with "getting it" in meditation didn't seem to be an issue at all for TM students. I found hundreds of thousands of reviews saying it was a life-changer—and while I wasn't looking for any more of that necessarily, I was looking for an escape.

We set off one morning on John's Harley. Nick had begged him to take the plunge in getting a bike, and they had since spent endless hours riding the winding and scenic routes around LA. That morning, John and I weaved in and out of the packed, trafficked lanes of the 101, arriving at our downtown orientation meeting sweaty and a bit disheveled.

That first meeting was a review of all the evidence-based research that revealed the biological benefits of meditation. If there were any doubters in the group at the outset of the meeting, there were none two hours later. It was impossible to not respect the heaps of research that proved the physiological and psychological benefits of meditation; the list included pretty much every aspect of well-being. We had three subsequent meetings, the most important one including a sacred and private moment where the instructor gave us our unique mantra, which, we were told, was never to be shared with anyone.

The use of a secret mantra is what distinguishes Transcendental Meditation from the many other forms of meditation that exist, all of which have their uniqueness and benefits. TM methodology doesn't use concentration to silence the mind's thoughts. Instead, by repeating the mantra silently, the process helps you transcend active thinking in order to reach a deep state of rest. Another great part about TM is that it doesn't require a silent spot to be in—the goal is not to quieten the world around you but instead to sink into and discover that quiet place within the chaos. In essence, you can reach your meditative state in any noisy, active place. This was perfect for our lifestyle, which at that time involved a house where we both worked from home and our homeschooled teenage musicians did too.

For those first few days, we were gently guided through a process that began with breathing, followed by the repetition of our mantra. "Don't force your thoughts away, just let them float through your mind. Don't judge them or the experience," our instructor had said. The only job we had was to repeat the mantra, slowly, over and over, for twenty minutes.

I don't know if there is something magical about the sacred mantra, but from that very first day onward, it worked. It was, indeed, a beeline to Zen. I started by saying my mantra and slowly felt as though I was sinking and sinking, as if beneath the sea. I felt a pressure, a small weight on my chest, as my breathing slowed down to a point where my heart seemed to beat at half its normal rate. It's the same to this day. While my conscious brain might be continuing to make my grocery list or think through a conversation or flip from one thought to another, another part of my being is gracefully disconnecting from this noise altogether, and from the "me" that is the noise.

Slowly I float, letting go, like a light and fluffy feather, allowing the release to a soundless place far, far away. In that place, there isn't a past or future—there are no expectations, obligations, or problems to find solutions to. There is no judgment of anything. The experience is incredibly restful, and when I come up, I am sometimes sad it's over. I want to go back.

The whole process is so perfectly satisfying—as though you are giving yourself, without any resistance, permission to naturally undo what you have so carefully put together. The identity, for a brief moment, is dropped, and all of the roles and responsibilities that go with it, and you can simply return to what was there at the start. There is much to be said about the concept of becoming, but also about unbecoming. Making the space for that to happen is like opening a window where the fresh air can blow in, and with it the possibility, a glimpse of clarity.

13

SILENT
SUFFERERS

DESPITE THE PROGRESS I was experiencing with this newfound voice of mine and our delving into meditation, I was being haunted by the growing, deepening body pain that had emerged soon after the earthquake. I now seemed to be suffering most of the time, and I noticed it seemed to worsen significantly around my monthly cycles. I decided to see my gynecologist.

"Adeno ... whaaattt?," I said to my OB as he was explaining the meaning of the streaky black marks on my ultrasound.

"Adenomyosis," he said slowly, as he spelled out the word on the back of a prescription pad. "It's a condition in which the inner lining of the uterus breaks through the muscle walls." He proceeded to sketch a diagram of my uterus, its muscles, then added the ovaries. The terms were all familiar to me, but at forty-five, I admitted to myself that I probably ought to have known more about the exact mechanics of the female system—especially as it was showing signs of malfunctioning.

I had made the appointment a few days before to see him, as I had noticed a link between my body pain and my cycles. With each passing month, they became increasingly longer and more excruciating. But the pain wasn't the normal type I had experienced over my lifetime, the few days of occasional cramping. This new experience was of a different genre altogether, as though it had tentacles that extended down my legs and into my feet. It was a deep, deep ache, sometimes accompanied by searing stabs that didn't come and go like normal menstrual cramps. It had endured initially for days, but then stretched to weeks on end, accompanied by a host of other symptoms—tremendous fatigue and a tenderness all over. In sum, it was like having the flu and being in labor all at once.

The change was so severe that it scared me and my doctor alike. Cancer was an obvious potential. "I had a patient in here yesterday with sudden changes not so dissimilar. We found out she had stage 4 ovarian cancer," he said flatly.

"Adenomyosis is not life-threatening," he continued.

"But the issue with it is that it is degenerative. It will only get worse until you complete menopause. Unfortunately, there are only two options—you can go on the pill to decrease the symptoms, or you can have a hysterectomy," he said bluntly.

I was relieved it wasn't something too serious, but I wasn't excited about knowing it would only get worse. In fact, I couldn't imagine the pain getting worse. I considered the options for treatment he had presented. I had read enough to know that any sort of extra hormone medication at this stage in my life could have serious negative effects; some experts thought taking the pill increases the risk of breast and cervical cancer. And a hysterectomy—no, I simply wasn't ready for that.

I went home and set out to learn everything I could about adenomyosis—the shadowy sister to the more commonly known endometriosis. I found dozens of website links and Facebook support groups of women who described nothing short of torment. Not only was I alarmed at the obvious number of women who were living with this, but I was also shocked at the lack of understanding from the medical community—what seemed to be a blatant acceptance of women needing to just put up with debilitating pain. Why was this so common yet I had never even heard of the term? Some called it the "hidden disease," and I felt a sudden and intense empathy for all of these women, referred to as the "silent sufferers," who were living quietly in such pain. I felt a kinship with them.

Interestingly though, there was little to learn online about the cause of it. Like fibroids and endometriosis, it was no doubt related to hormones, but what caused the onset of the condition was unclear to most. Several articles made the relation to an over-production of estrogen. *And what caused that?* I wondered. Our diets are now full of elements stimulating the imbalance—everything from soy products to toxins from plastic bottles. But I also found a huge body of evidence that referenced the imbalances stemming from stress. Winding further down roads of research, I read that it could be caused by the daily type of stress or a more sudden type from trauma or shock.

Hmmm, I wondered. The symptoms were coming on the heels of what had been the scariest experience of my life in Nepal. Since that day, I had felt different in so many ways, both good and bad, like an awakening and a degeneration at the same time. It was as if bells were going off in my body; some were loud and alarming, like this terrible pain, and others were more like the tinkling of wind chimes, signaling me, nudging me, to let go, to open up to something new. But the connection between the experience in Nepal and this ugly condition was less than concrete. Maybe it all came down to drinking from plastic bottles—who knew.

One day I was with Emma at the Korean Spa in downtown Los Angeles. We had made it a bit of a ritual to go on a Sunday. Located in the dark basement of a downtown building on Wilshire Boulevard, it was as though the world ceased to exist as women, all naked and mostly Korean, went about the steamy rooms, scrubbing themselves, scrubbing each other, and catching up on the week's happenings. It was easy to get over being self-conscious, as women of all shapes and sizes sauntered around comfortably.

On one particular day, the woman sitting next to me in the steam bath struck up a conversation. When the air cleared a bit, I noticed she had had a double mastectomy. Before long she was telling me the story of how she had survived breast cancer without any radiation or chemotherapy. "I went the all-natural Chinese herb route," she explained. "Dr. Chi in Orange County is one of the best herbalists in the country. He taught me how most female reproductive issues, especially cancers, are related to an overproduction of estrogen in the body. Left untreated, they rapidly lead to cancer. He put me on a rigid diet of no sugar, no fruit, no red meat, dairy, or soy—oh and a ton of various herbs. It was really hard but I am so excited to say that after one year of seeing him and following his routine, I became cancer-free. I still wanted to remove my breasts for prevention, and it was an uphill battle convincing my doctors to go ahead with it, as I was cancer-free."

I shared with her what I was living with and that I had also seen a link between estrogen production and adenomyosis.

"Go," she said, "I am sure he can help."

A few weeks later, I was in Dr. Chi's office. He looked at my tongue, he held my hand and inspected the half-moons on my fingernails. He considered the small red spots I had all over my chest.

"Estrogen problem," he said in his thick Chinese accent. "All pre-cancer signs."

He prescribed the same diet as my friend from the spa had described, and I was given a host of herbal supplements—ones to increase my *chi*, the Chinese term for life force. According to him, my weakened chi resulted in poor circulation, which in turn created a domino effect on the entire balance of my system.

"Do this for about a year and you will get well," he said. "No birth control, no hysterectomy."

A year? A year without sugar, fruit, meat, or dairy? Good god. How will I survive this?

"When will I know if I am better?" I asked.

"When your symptoms are gone," he said, then sent me off.

I was amazed at the difference in approach between Dr. Chi and what my own gynecologist had outlined as my only two options for relief. Like the indigenous medicinal practices of the Maya, traditional Chinese medicine sought balance and restoration through the body's chi. It, too, approached health holistically, using natural herbs in the healing process.

I religiously stuck to the routine, privately and silently waiting for signs of change. Only my inner circle of family and friends knew the torment of pain that I was experiencing. It was strange to have to explain the weird and sudden diet, let alone this condition that nobody had heard of, and I kept it as hidden as I could. I didn't want to talk about it—didn't want to share it. Somewhere deep down, I was ashamed of it.

Month after month, I prayed that I would feel better, but with each cycle, I dove deeper into a dark hole of wretchedness. My only escape was work and meditation. Everything in between was a living hell. Thank God I had the luxury of working from home, where I would prop myself up on the couch and attempt to lose myself in the day's workload—it was my drug. I trained my brain to think only of what was in front of me—anything other than what was going on inside of me, the black hole that felt like labor, day in and day out, night after night. I began to focus on the calendar, pinpointing the rapidly diminishing few days when I might be pain-free.

I will never forget getting down to six days out of thirty that I felt OK. But I am a firm believer that important lessons always line our difficult periods, and looking back, there were several for me. When I finally reached the day when I had no pain, no hemorrhaging, and no fatigue, I would wake up and know that it was going to be a beautiful, magical day—and I treasured it like the holy grail. It was like someone had flicked a switch and miraculously turned off the nightmare. On those days, the light was brighter, the sky bluer. I would pack as much into those twenty-four hours as I possibly could, beginning with walks in the canyon I normally could no longer manage. I happily took care of normal errands, grocery shopping, and folding laundry. The most mundane activities became sheer, utter pleasure. On those rare and precious pain-free days, I taught myself to slow time down, to soak in and embrace every. single. second.

14

RED-LIGHT
REALITY

IN THE SPRING OF 2016, GoPhil offered a journey to Nepal—the focus of which centered around both the obstacles and the progress communities faced in rebuilding their homes and lives. We had continued to commit to a small number of NGOs that were addressing large-scale emergency needs on a shoestring. Money from the government, promised to everyone who had lost or damaged homes, had only begun to trickle in. Construction projects were proving difficult, as there was a dire need to implement earthquake-resistant building techniques; everyone seemed the expert, especially the international community, yet the Nepali people were still distrustful of the ground beneath them. It was clear this was going to take time and patience and a delicate combination of managing the resources within Nepal and those offered from outside.

As a foundation, we had always felt it was important to include our donors in our work. Other nonprofit organizations saw them as check-writers, but we considered them to be valuable well beyond what they contributed financially. And, we thought, the more they understood the context surrounding the work of the NGOs, the better our partnerships could be in the long term. It had been twelve months since the earthquake, and a lot of work had transpired with the organizations we were supporting. We felt it was time to visit in person. Since I had been involved in the early stages of our expansion to Nepal, acting as the point person for our relief efforts, it seemed only natural for me to guide the trip.

We were also overdue to offer a journey to India. As Nepal and India share a border, we thought it made sense to run the trips back to back, hitting two birds with one stone by being in the region and giving travelers the opportunity to visit both countries.

I didn't think much about whether the moment was right for me to go. A year had seemed a sufficient amount of time for me to be able to move on from some of the initial shock. I was aware of my lingering insecurities but was also consumed with the work we were involved in, and I was eager and anxious to get back. My only big hesitation was that I physically might not be in the best shape to handle the back-to-back trips. I mulled it over for a couple of weeks and came to the conclusion that I would will myself to do it—to push through it, come hell or high water, as I had done so many times before.

A wonderful small group of dynamic women registered for the first leg to New Delhi. Anne Elgerd, a veteran GoPhil donor and community member, joined—she would later become GoPhil's board chair. Anne and I had shared many of life passions over the years, and expanding the potential that resided at the grassroots was one of them. It would be her third journey to visit our NGO partners in India. Anne possessed what I always considered a highly tuned moral compass. She was a deep listener and, as a result, often picked up on the subtle energies most people missed. Jane and Samantha, a mother-daughter pair, had also signed up. They were both passionate advocates for our partners working against gender-based violence. I was also thrilled to have my sister, Helene, come along. She had watched GoPhil grow from an idea to a thriving reality, and I was excited to share the inner workings with her.

Our group was scheduled to visit three of our New Delhi partners, each working on a range of issues relating to the protection of vulnerable women and children. Our first stop was to visit the formidable Lalitha who directed the SMS Center for Children located on GB Road in the red-light district of Delhi. GB Road houses brothels where an estimated four thousand sex workers, most of whom have been trafficked, are forced to live in bonded labor, at times with their children. Lalitha opened the center after learning about the desperate futures these women faced along-side their children, who sat, all too often, at the foot of the beds as their mothers were forced to perform their duties with men. Girls would be particularly at risk for a life much the same. To break the intergenerational cycle of forced prostitution would take immense effort. Lalitha's center provided these at-risk children with an education, their only chance at a life outside GB Road, and a safe and secure environment in which to sleep. And most importantly, the center offered these children the care they needed while also remaining in close contact with their mothers, who faced the daily nightmare behind the barred windows of the brothels.

Visiting Delhi's red-light district is not an altogether safe outing—approximately ninety-five percent of the prostitutes have been trafficked to the district; as a result, the comings and goings are tracked carefully by those managing the highly lucrative and corrupt business. Police, journalists, foreigners, and any other form of outsider are not welcomed in this controlled environment. Given the risks to personal safety, it has been a challenge for Lalitha to retain qualified staff willing to work at the center.

We slipped discreetly from our cars and walked the few steps through the door of the center, which was immediately closed and locked behind us. "Welcome, welcome!" beamed Lalitha as she hugged me tightly, greeting each one in our group with equal warmth. The entranceway was abuzz with children lining up to go to school. "It's exam time, so they are a little nervous. Come, come!" she said excitedly as she ushered us into a small room where chairs had been neatly arranged for our visit.

Facilitating onsite visits with our partner programs continues to be one of the most magical, transformational aspects of our work at GoPhil. It is in these moments that we gain a profound appreciation for the complex nature that their work involves, but we can also feel the passion, tenacity, and resourcefulness required to keep it going in the harshest of environments, like GB Road. Having the time to listen to what sparked the beginnings, what inspired the founders of these organizations to respond to a great call to action, all too often rooted in injustice, provides the soil for our ability to understand. This understanding makes us better able to listen more fully, and when we do, we cannot help but want to do our part. It's as if the listening becomes the catalyst for our own action.

But philanthropic travel can be fraught with unforeseen nuances and unintended consequences—we have learned some beautiful yet harsh lessons over the years. Bringing these two worlds together, even with the purest of intentions, has the power to divide as much as it can unite us. It requires thoughtful planning and a careful awareness of expectations that can be present on both sides: the partner and the visitor. We often overlook the power and influence that come with offering funding, and both sides need to be aware of how this can show up, especially onsite.

One of the most common risks in combining giving and travel, also prevalent with volunteering trips, is a tendency for a visitor to look from the outside in with foreign eyes, blurry with long hours of travel, and make assumptions about what an organization might need. While visitors to developing countries typically have been given greater access to life's abundance—education, opportunities, and financial resources—this position of privilege does not make us capable of understanding and solving the unique problems that communities are addressing. This falls into a broader yet common presumption that donors know what is best. In fact, we possess only a limited perspective of the economic, cultural, historical, and social backdrops at play. It's actually quite ludicrous, arrogant even, to think we are in a position of knowing more than those who live with these challenges each day.

If we aren't aware and extremely thoughtful in these situations, we can also find power and influence showing up when a program feels the need to prove its worth to secure future funding, or when a donor is looking for recognition or gratitude for their support. Any length of time working alongside these programs will reveal who is doing the hard work in the equation—who needs to be thanked. While I firmly believe we need all hands, heads, and hearts on deck to solve the global issues of our time, we should remain acutely aware, as we board our airplanes, of who continues to contribute, to give, and to invest a thousandfold when we return home.

How these subtle undercurrents intersect during donor journeys can make for an awkward dance at times, and we'll admit that we have learned each and every lesson the hard way. In our early days, we allowed travelers to hand out gifts to children, reinforcing a "giver and receiver" relationship and a Western savior narrative. We didn't protect the right to privacy by placing limitations on taking photographs. Luckily, those days are long gone, and we now see our role as a facilitator in what we feel is a very enlightening experience—and we take it very seriously. Bringing people together from different places in life requires a sacred space—one in which respect, humility, and dignity need to remain at the center. What happens from this place can be a beautiful journey in itself, for each person involved, but it also requires an unwavering commitment to values and a fair amount of preparation before the journey even begins.

Sitting there in front of Lalitha on that hot and dusty New Delhi morning, we couldn't help but be drawn into her world. On a small projector screen, she carefully showed us a map they created for outreach. It revealed the layout of the brothels—there were one hundred in all. Young girls were sold into prostitution for the equivalent of about seven hundred US dollars. They came from India, Bangladesh, and Nepal, and most of them would never return home. Impressively, out of the two thousand children that had come through the SMS center over the years, not one of them had followed in their mothers' footsteps. On the contrary, many had gone on to attend university and pursue careers in social work, software engineering, health care, and more.

The needs at the SMS center were basic and critical—they desperately wanted to offer the children better nutritional oversight, more protein and nutrients, than they were able to provide. They were lacking a social worker who could track the case files of the children more closely. And the kids needed outings to expand their minds and offer them a window outside of the misery of GB Road. GoPhil donors had given generously to the center over the years, but Lalitha explained how funding was only a part of what is needed for small NGOs to survive long term. GoPhil's model of investment took this into account. Spinning several plates at one time, Lalitha had been struggling in several operational areas of running the center. Knowing that we couldn't provide her with the specific contextual knowledge that her work involved, we arranged for Priti Patkar, the co-founder and director of the organization Prerana, a pioneer in protecting vulnerable children in the red-light districts of Mumbai, to mentor her over the course of a year. In addition, we had funded workshops led by local experts to help programs like SMS in fundraising and resource mobilization. Being aware of these varying needs required regular and honest dialogue. Emily Bild, GoPhil's Director of Global Programs is vigilant in keeping these crucial conversations going as without them we wouldn't have the insight needed to be a good partner.

The clanging of pots and pans and the honking of traffic outside made its way through the barred windows near where we sat, fixated on her words that described another world, one where the hope and hard work that emerged from within the walls of the SMS center changed the course of children's lives every day.

Mindful of the precious time and energy it took to host us, we didn't stay too long. We said goodbye to Lalitha and the staff, quietly retreating to our cars that had waited to take us out of the prison streets of GB Road. None of us said much on the ride, all of us perhaps privately asking ourselves how it was that the world was so unfair to some and not to others. We visited two other programs over the course of the next few days while also weaving in some fun and sightseeing, but even in those lighter moments, you could tell that everyone was processing big questions. No matter what efforts we were making through GoPhilanthropic, we were able to leave the ugly realities; I always left wondering if we were doing enough, whether there were opportunities we were not seeing.

Things started to get challenging one night. "Helene—clear out!" I yelled as I ran to the bathroom. "I can't clear out, Lyd—I'm in here and not feeling so well!" she yelled back. It was a small hotel, but I had no idea just how small until we could literally hear the cacophony of noises coming from each other's rooms—all night long. We all had suddenly fallen pretty sick, most likely from the lunch we had eaten earlier that day. We crawled to the breakfast table the following morning, each of us in a terrible state. Trips always include a risk of sickness but rarely does everyone go down at once.

I knew I had to be on my game to guide the next leg, and luckily, I bounced back pretty quickly, but the others suffered terribly with ongoing stomach issues. All of us were traveling on to Nepal except Helene, who limped home and was sick for another two weeks. I had loved being with her and was sad to see her go. "It was so good to see you in your element, Lyd—I don't know where you get your energy. It's like you have an endless source of it when you are doing this."

She was right. Since arriving, I had felt nothing but a surge of wonderful energy, stomach problems and all. It was such a contrast to how I had felt over the previous months. My heart was full and my mind engaged in all there was to do. I was back in drive mode and it felt good. But as we walked to the gate at the Delhi airport where we awaited our flight to Kathmandu, I felt my strength drain with every step. The spirit that had been running through me so naturally in Delhi was being replaced by fear and insecurity— slowly they crept in and claimed their space.

Wanting to hide my unsettled feelings, I found a seat a few rows away from the rest of the group to try and shake it off. A few minutes later, I felt a warm hand on my back. I turned and found solace in Anne's caring smile and then her warm embrace—she knew going back to Nepal would be difficult. I took a couple of deep breaths as I felt tears run down my face. "There is so much to be done, Anne—we must continue to do something important, and it is way more important than whatever it is I am afraid of, whatever that is," I said, hoping to convince myself of my own words. She gave my shoulder a little squeeze and then just sat beside me, transmitting a calm simply with her presence.

As the plane descended into Kathmandu, I tried to get to the source of the fear. Did I think there could be another earthquake?

Was I worried about the flood of memories? No. Neither got to the heart of what was roaming around my consciousness. I couldn't quite find the answer—maybe it would become clearer over the coming days. Then a familiar, bitter voice made its way across my mind. *There is a lot wrong with what is down there on that ground. There is no way to make any of it right—what you have, who you are, is not enough. It will never be enough.*

15

RETURN

Our deepest fear is not that we are inadequate. Our deepest fear is that we are powerful beyond measure. It is our light, not our darkness, that most frightens us.

—Marianne Williamson

MY HEART STARTED TO POUND as the plane descended. It pounded even harder as we stepped off the plane and into the warm, moist air. Inhaling, I felt a metallic taste spread over the inside of my mouth. Sweat dripped from under my arms as we stood, for what felt like an eternity, in the customs line. Hours later, we settled into a simple yet lovely boutique hotel in Thamel, the popular tourist area of the city.

I sat on my little porch overlooking the red-bricked court-yard, prayer flags flapping in the wind. There on the corner of the wall was a small, singular prayer wheel. I could feel myself calming just from gazing at it. It was then that I heard another internal voice, a different one, and from a place I knew I could trust.

You have a job to do and fear has no role in it, the voice said with no uncertain terms. *You can feel vulnerable—completely and utterly vulnerable. This might make you feel small, like you want to become invisible, but you are not to fear anything. Fear is just the absence of light. Carry the light within you—that's all you are asked to do. Bring that to the table. It is enough.*

And then I remembered a lesson Arun Gandhi had shared with me when he was mourning the loss of his grandfather Mahatma Gandhi and the responsibility he felt to walk in enormous shoes. He had helped me understand that our purpose wasn't necessarily about seeking perfection or making things right, but to find the light within us that we each had—and with it, to cast it on the path before us. Even in my darkest moments, I had felt that light inside me, and that included the days when the flame was dull or nearly nonexistent. *OK*, I thought. *I think I can do this.* Behind these uncertain feelings that my efforts, that our efforts and support, were only a drop in a sea of need, sat another thought, a bigger knowing. Every single bit of care helped—even the smallest acts of kindness mattered. And it wasn't the job of one to care—it was the job of many.

Five additional GoPhil travelers joined us in Nepal. We settled into our hotel, and I met up with Lilu KC, a Nepalese woman who had taken on the role of program liaison for GoPhil. Lilu had been a valuable addition to our team. She was not only bright and compassionate, but with no cultural divides to face, as we often did, Lilu could capture the challenges and priorities of our programs more easily. They trusted her and shared their candid thoughts and ideas with less inhibition. This experience was a critical moment for us as we began to see that, despite our intense desire to help, our presence as foreigners could be a true barrier.

While the group got settled, Lilu and I met with Raj and Steve, both of whom would be guiding various parts of the journey. It was lovely to see them again; we hadn't parted in the best of circumstances during the earthquake, and it had been a hard year for them both—physically, mentally, and economically. "You'll need to manage the expectations of your group, Lydia," Raj warned. "We are only just opening up here and things won't always run smoothly. We are still recovering in every way."

To make matters worse, after the earthquake, Nepal was confronted with issues surrounding the approval of a much-needed Constitution, which had been in the works since the abolishment of their monarchy in 2008. The new document became controversial, flaring tensions between local communities, namely those who lived on the border of India, the heart of Nepal's trade route. A border blockade had ensued, stopping fuel and other key supplies from flowing into an already struggling country. It was a complex issue involving a myriad of socioeconomic, political, and systemic forces at work. Outside looking in, it was as if Nepal was in the ring, facing one big blow after another.

As we made our way across town in a sea of thick and dusty traffic, I realized Raj hadn't exaggerated. There didn't appear to be any evidence of rebuilding—anywhere. Streets were lined with piles of rubble; destroyed buildings sat in heaps. Rows and rows of emergency relief tents blanketed the city, indicating where families were still living and would continue to live for a long time. Half an hour later, we arrived at Karma Coffee, a unique little social enterprise café run by Raj's wife, Birgit. It's where we were due to meet with Martin Punaks, the country director for Next Generation Nepal (NGN). For years, NGN had been working on the front lines, rescuing and reunifying children from the corrupt orphanages where they had been trafficked.

For the next two hours, we sat engrossed as he explained the realities of an unground business fueled by Western do-good intention.

"It's essentially a food chain, and here's how it works. Traffickers go into the poor mountainous areas where ethnic groups are uneducated, and they take a fee from parents to bring their children to Kathmandu where they promise to give them an education. They bring the children to an orphanage where they give them a "fake orphan story" to tell, along with phony papers. The orphanage then solicits donations from well-meaning volunteers or visitors. Oftentimes, the children are deliberately malnourished to raise funds. There is money to be made on both ends, so it's a very attractive and lucrative business," he explained.

Martin went on to describe how there were over six hundred children's homes in Kathmandu. "And these are only the legal ones; there are many more that are unregistered. Eighty percent of them are located in the top tourist districts, which shows the direct link to tourism," he said flatly.

Once children had been rescued, which was, in itself, a long and complex process that involved the Central Child Welfare Board as well as the police, it could take months, or in the hardest of cases, even one to two years to reunite with their families. Like NGN, GoPhil believed in the growing movement toward deinstitutionalization—better known as DI in the development world. Years of research had proven that institutionalized care should be a last resort for a child—that children were more likely to thrive, even in poor conditions, in the care of their family networks. Shifting funding from orphanages and shelters to strengthening families and communities was key to ensuring that children didn't find themselves being raised in institutions. Unfortunately, the earthquake had only destabilized remote villages and marginalized communities even more. Traffickers had been exploiting the situation ever since.

The presentation was a shocking eye-opener for our group. Western desire to want to fix a problem when uninformed on so many levels was, in fact, causing incredible harm to children. And to this day, it is still a relatively unknown phenomena. We continue to encourage our young adults, in particular, who might not know much of the world just yet, to volunteer at orphanages, and better yet—raise funds for them. It looks good on the college application.

Rishi Bhandari, a Nepali who grew up surrounded by international volunteers, succinctly explains the broader problem of exoticism of volunteering. "It all comes down to the subtle effects of colonialism. The Western kids grow up with the idea that they can do anything—that they can come to another place and teach anything, build anything, offer anything. And Nepali society is somehow brainwashed into believing that these teenagers really do know what they are doing. The cumulative impact of this can be really tiring. ... People from underserved communities are then taught that they need it [this help], then they are influenced in being grateful for it." It was just one of many examples of the need to rethink how we go about channeling our desire to make a difference.

"Martin—thank you so much. It's a hard job to burst the bubble—to explain that giving, that helping, can hurt, but it's so important. We must continue to educate, to help people question our limited perspectives—to work on creating the better pathways to leverage our resources in ways that will address the root causes of these problems, not create more," I said on my way out.

Knowing the girls home in Dhulikhel I had visited was most likely the result of the same food chain continued to make me ill. Martin had been the first person I had contacted after returning from Nepal in 2015. He had helped me understand that the possibilities of getting to the bottom of it would be slim, to not get my hopes up. "Lydia—there are hundreds and hundreds of homes like this all over the city. You can't imagine the work it takes to investigate, let alone get to the point of rescuing and reuniting them with their families."

I knew he was right. In the year since, I hadn't made any headway on a possible investigation, especially with the focus being shifted to relief efforts. In a normal year, it would take months to line up the proper organizations. But I wasn't going to allow these realities to stop me from hoping, from believing, from at least trying. I made an internal vow to forge on, however long it took.

We spent the next few days visiting GoPhil's other partners around the city. We piled into the back of a pickup truck and wound our way to the village of Dadaguan, where we had collaborated with other funders to purchase a brick-making machine for the villagers to use themselves. They had made some successful attempts at making bricks but were not yet confident in their mixture of sand to cement. As a result, they had yet to rebuild even one of the seventy homes that had been leveled in the disaster.

Dhorje, the school principal, had found success in making a few bricks that he felt good about, and they were lined up neatly on the ground. But the villagers as a whole didn't share the same confidence and would not plough full steam ahead until they knew they could count on each and every brick with their lives. Families were patiently making do living underneath makeshift tarps and corrugated sheeting until they got it just right. While the daily struggles were evident, it was clear they were managing their project on their own terms.

At the end of the trip, most of the group branched off to do some trekking, Anne carrying the baton as trip director while I stayed back to have more detailed meetings with the programs. After finishing earlier than expected one afternoon, I took a taxi to Dwarika's—it had been on my mind since arriving to return to where I been during the earthquake, yet I hadn't yet found the right quiet moment to go. With the days dwindling quickly, I knew it had to be done.

Getting out of the taxi, I almost turned to tell him to wait, that I would only be a couple of minutes, but I stopped myself, knowing that it wouldn't do it justice. I pushed open the oversized wooden door and walked into the cool bricked courtyard, the sound of water trickling in the background. The smell in the air, a mixture of incense, wood, and stone, was immediately familiar.

Guests were milling around relaxed and happy, lounging in the sun and on the big wooden daybeds. Children, wet from swimming, were wrapped in the same white-and-blue-striped towels that we had used as blankets. I took small steps, making my way to the back terrace. There I found the two trees, swaying easily in the breeze, green with new growth. Next to them were the rows of prayer wheels that had stood vigil on that rainy night.

I sat down on a wooden bench for some time, taking in the warmth of the sun and the sound of the chirping birds flying in and out of the courtyard. It was peaceful, and I felt comforted. I thought about all I had been shown since that day. The earth and sky had spoken often and in so many different ways—from the purest energy I had felt in the natural world, to the quiet I had discovered inside myself from meditation. I had sensed it in the wind and in the moonlit sky and from the white feathers that I would find along the path, reminding me I was connected to something big, something whole.

It's all here, everything you need is within you and around you, it had said. I knew there was much more to it and more to understand; it was only the beginning, only the start of communicating with life in a different way, but I felt satisfied in knowing that I was awake. I was listening. There was nowhere to go, and no need to run.

On my way out of the hotel, I noticed a massive board, a whole wall displaying pictures of a temporary shelter called "Camp Hope" that the Dwarika Foundation was funding for hundreds of villagers from Sindhupalchowk, one of Nepal's most devastated regions. In the photos, I noticed images of Shrestha Des, the daughter of Des, the original owner, the striking and sure-footed woman who had so bravely navigated and cared for everyone in her hotel as the walls of the city came down.

Just as I was turning to leave, I saw her sitting at a table with some hotel guests. She was as radiant and confident as I had remembered, and I knew in that moment that I needed to speak to her, to thank her for being so strong, for keeping us all safe. I waited, uncomfortably, until she was done speaking with the people around her. When she had finished, I approached her and introduced myself.

"Hello, my name is Lydia Dean. I was here during the earthquake last year—I was one of the first to leave the following day. I just wanted to say thank you. Thank you for caring for all of us—you did it with such grace." The word tumbled out of my mouth without even thinking about it, yet as it did, I understood why I had admired her so. She had, without flinching, responded so courageously, standing up to the task, to what was being asked of her in the painful moment, and for the months following. What I also felt, but didn't express, was the gratitude I carried for the love and thought that her father had put into building the walls of Dwarika. His passion for preserving their heritage had stood the test of time and all of its trials.

She squinted her eyes as if trying to remember me. "Ah ... those were some hard days. We stayed open and provided shelter to guests for many, many days after, but at some point, we had to close. I hadn't slept for a week," she said. We then spent time talking about her ongoing efforts with Camp Hope. She asked me what I was doing in Nepal. Her eyes lit up and a warmth came over her as I explained the details of our partnerships. They were small efforts on the grand scheme of what was needed, but they represented something positive—that people on the other side of the earth cared. They didn't forget twelve months later. We shook hands, and I left the hotel feeling deeply relieved, as if I had replaced the traumatic memories with hope and the motivation to continue to walk forward. I could carry on with wherever life was taking me, knowing that I, too, possessed the strength to respond to what it would ask of me.

The group returned from their trek, tired and disappointed. Their flight to Pokhara had been delayed for many hours due to poor air visibility caused by pollution. The logistics of the trek had not gone smoothly, and everyone was ready to go home. For some, Nepal had not been what they were expecting. It hadn't helped that within twelve hours of arriving in Kathmandu, whatever illness we had picked up in India had made its way through the rest of the group. The combination of touring a country in such a fragile state and guiding a group that was not physically well had me questioning whether it had been a good idea to come. While it had been important to contribute to kickstarting the tourism industry the country greatly relied upon, the timing of the journey had felt off. The pleaser in me felt somehow responsible for not meeting expectations, but something else was at work, and the protective mother side of me understood this to be more important. Nepal was still healing. It needed time to focus inward, to care for itself, before it could shine its light brightly again.

16

HOME

"DO YOU REALLY THINK WE SHOULD DO IT? Is it too soon? Gosh—Emma is still pretty young," I said worriedly as we marched up the steep rocky path in the hills behind our house in Provence. It was spring and the wildflowers were just waking from their winter sleep. The air was fresh and thick with aroma— flowering thyme and rosemary.

"Lyd— ask yourself what you were doing at this age. Weren't we all getting on with our lives beyond our parents at age eighteen?" John responded.

"You don't understand—you aren't a mother," I snapped back unfairly. The thought of leaving the children was like sticking my finger in a raging fire.

We had been kicking around the idea of moving back to France for some time, to where life always felt clearer and more grounded, but the conversations were muddy and rife with emotions, and I always ended up in tears. But one element was never questioned, never interpreted in different ways, never argued about. Provence was also the closest we had ever come to calling a place home.

In 2001, we had left the US, confused about the trajectory we were on and needing a timeout. We had been working as self-employed executive search consultants, and within a short span, had found ourselves in a vortex of stress, success, and consumption. I hit the stop button as if my life depended on it and quit working to stay at home with the children. I needed to think. I needed to read. And when I had done enough of that, I wanted to escape, to leave—to travel the world and find something useful to do in it.

John realized there was no turning back—a switch had been flicked and Plan B was in order. My father had a three-hundred-year-old village house in the small town of Rognes, twenty-five minutes outside of the ancient Papal city of Aix-en-Provence. We could rent it for a year and figure ourselves out from there.

From the minute our family's feet hit the earth in Provence, we discovered a rhythm we had yet to experience together—and it just felt right. The kids went to school with the local children, soaking in the French and the natural Provencal culture easily. We found Mas de Gancel, an abandoned old folks' home with a small vineyard, and spent the following year learning the language and restoring her into a cozy haven. When it was finished, we rented it out during the peak summer weeks to tourists, as we had with our house in Costa Rica, and lived as simply as we could on the rental income for the rest of the year, traveling to many of the places I had dreamed of visiting.

It was a near-idyllic seven years—like a big, long sigh, a much-needed exhale, from being wound so tight we didn't know who we were or what we wanted. In Provence, time was our own, and little by little, we discovered what we loved to do. It was as simple as that. But there was also something unique to the region that I felt was embedded in the richness of the soil—a restorative ingredient that sunk into your body and your soul. Provence was earthiness and fertile, dripping with perfect fruit and wine, and full of rolling fields of bright and vibrant flowers, from poppies to sunflowers and lavender. We have heard it a million times from visitors: food tastes better here; sleeps are deeper. Net sum, Provence is abundant. It gives itself to you at every turn, and it feels very good, like a healthy, nurturing drug.

But by the time Izzy had arrived from China, we were faced with realistic pressures to return back to the US. She had been born with fibular hemimelia, a congenital birth condition that caused a significant limb difference, and it was demanding more medical options than we had near us. Nick and Emma were at a stage where English classes were in order, should they want to attend universities outside France. For us, we had been floating year to year on what we earned from renting the house to tourists, and this wasn't providing the financial security we felt we needed for the future as a family. We were all torn in leaving, but it had been such a beautiful period of our lives, we didn't feel right in asking for more.

Keeping our house as a rental property was an easy way to cling to the memories of our life there. We also rented instead of buying our homes in the US, returning several times a year to Mas de Gancel for all of the major holidays and to build the expanding villa business. This one-foot-in-and-one-foot-out model worked, but the problem was that our beloved home, the place where we kept our wedding photos, the pieces of furniture that had been passed down from generations, the place where we wrapped ourselves up in the comfort of what was familiar and known, wasn't a place where we could live anymore. Instead, we shared it with strangers. We could come for ten-day stints, most of which we would spend jetlagged, and I would return back to the US as though I had left a part of myself back in Provence. I felt as if I had severed my roots.

As Nick reached twenty and Emma graduated from high school, we felt the timing could be right to resume a life back in France. The only Provence rental business was thriving, with over two hundred properties on its site; but more and more, John felt himself disconnected from the source of his passion. He wanted to expand on his love and knowledge of real estate, particularly old homes, and had a dream of developing a real estate sales and renovation company. It would be called Provence Life.

For me, the return to Provence had to do with something deeper, more fundamental. While our first move to France was about exploring and finding meaning and purpose in life, this need to go back had to do with a profound desire to reflect and to heal—not just from the last shaky couple of years, but from all that life had presented to me thus far. I longed to return home, yet somewhere in my mind, I knew this word went beyond the four walls at Mas de Gancel. I needed to continue to discover something in myself, and I had a strong feeling that Provence, with its magical light and rich earth, held the space for that to happen.

Nick made some of the early discussions easier on me. He was ready to branch out on his own and live independently. "I have been given such a great foundation—you guys have been there to help me since the beginning. I almost feel as if I need to be on my own to know if I can really do it," he admitted one day. "I want to feel as though I only have myself to lean on—if you are both by my side all of the time, I will never dig down to find it in myself."

The words stung, not because I was angry in hearing them, but because I knew he was right. I wanted nothing other than to hold the kids in my arms for the rest of my waking days, but I knew that letting go, and creating space for them to discover all that they had within them, was what needed to happen. Nick chose not to go to university, instead immersing himself in a world of creativity—learning from a vast range of musicians, producers, photographers, and filmmakers. Emma, who was two years younger, was naturally one or two steps behind in her readiness to fly solo. She had made the difficult decision to not pursue a career in music—it had been a grueling choice, but she knew, despite her talent, that it wasn't her lifelong mission. She had spent so much of her time in recording studios that she had missed the opportunity to take her ACT and SAT. By the time she graduated, attending a local community college seemed the logical step.

For a family that had been glued together in lockstep since the day we decided to spend a summer in Costa Rica so many years before, it was strange terrain to find ourselves at a place of separation. We had made a home in Provence, traveled widely, and had exceptional experiences together, and we all knew deep down that it was time for a new chapter. Nick and Emma moved into an apartment together in Brentwood on the Westside of LA, and John, Iz, and I flew over the great pond.

We settled back into Mas de Gancel and slowly reconnected with the life we had cherished. We took long walks in the hills near the house, behind the Roman ruins at Chateau Bas and up to the crumbled remains of Vernègues. We ate at our favorite crèperie Le Repaire on the top of the hill, savoring their simple salads and local rosé. We enrolled Isabelle at IBS, an International School outside of Aix. It was too far to drive each day, so she boarded in a small house with other children from all around the world for four days a week. John began the long road in building yet another business—a task mired with administrative hassles and endless paperwork, yet his love for old homes and transforming them, giving them new life, helped him see through the hurdles.

I resumed my normal routine with GoPhil, this time from an old wooden desk that looked out from underneath the wisteria-covered terrace and on to the vineyard. I spent my mornings catching up on emails, reading reports, and writing to donors about the goings-on in all of the programs. Being in a different time zone meant the Skype calls began late in the afternoon, sometimes lasting through early evening. In moving back, somehow my day had become even longer. When the sun set, we lit candles and roaring fires and sat as we had always done, eating cross-legged around the coffee table in front of the fireplace.

We spoke with Nick and Emma several times a week on FaceTime. They were doing well on their own yet logically had their wobbly moments. Nick's career continued to bring tremendous highs and lows—we never knew what to expect when we looked at our phones in the morning. "You'll never believe it—I had the most amazing meeting with Atlantic Records. They say they want to sign!" And another day, "My manager quit—just like that. He just threw in the towel. I don't know what I'm going to do. I'm back to square one." He was devastated for what felt like the millionth time in his young career. And Emma, struggled in her own way, as she faced making more decisions on her own.

These were normal growing pains for young adults, but I would go to bed with a heavy heart, tossing and turning, worrying as mothers all around the planet do, about how to make life easier for their children—how to ease their problems and take away their hardships. I was terribly uncomfortable with the thought of them facing pain in any way.

And then there was my own pain. Mine. Despite all my efforts, it had endured. I had stayed with my Dr. Chi diet—removing any speck of sugar, meat, fruit, or dairy from my diet, but the deep endless aching had persisted. It's amazing how we think our problems might miraculously disappear when we physically transport ourselves across an ocean. They have this annoying way of clinging to our backs until we are ready to face them.

The only relief I found was through treatments by a local man, Cezar, who had been trained by his grandfather in an ancient practice called magnetism. Like reiki, blocked energy is released when a healer moves his hands slowly above the chakras. Cezar would hover his hands over my body, and I could literally feel the heat, his energy, untie bundles of knots. They weren't muscular knots—it was as if he was undoing, releasing emotional knots within my cells. "Tu est vide Lydia—épuisée (*You are empty—void of energy*)," he would say at the outset of our sessions. It wasn't surprising; I was traveling more than ever now that we were in France. I would go west to see the kids, my parents, and for GoPhil events, and I would go east to see the programs, whenever I could. While nobody was near, I felt comfortably sandwiched between the two. The only downside was a very full, too full schedule that involved a lot of doing and a lot of movement. No wonder I lacked energy. But stepping out into the crisp air after a session with Cezar, I had the sensation of being plugged into a warm energy socket. Refueled, I would walk home ready to take on the world again.

17

LES AGNELS

There are only two ways to live your life. One is as though nothing is a miracle. The other is as though everything is.

—Laura Lynne Jackson

MOVING BACK TO FRANCE felt like a step closer to something fundamental, like I was fumbling my way back to where I was meant to be. But our plan involved one small snag, and that was where we would live during the weeks Mas de Gancel was rented. The cost of maintaining the house required that we keep running it as a vacation rental, and visitors started coming in during the early spring weeks and continued through the fall. In a good rental season, we could be out of the house close to six months of the year, and this was a significant amount of time to be displaced. The home we had dreamed of returning to was, in fact, an idyllic concept. Reality looked different, and it involved moving from here to there week to week.

John and I argued endlessly about it. I wanted to just live in it—to have it as ours and only ours—all year long. I was done with sharing my sacred space, done with knowing strangers slept in my bed. But the numbers never seemed to make logical financial sense, and I was hard-pressed to justify my own argument. We knew it was time to look for a place we could call our own.

"I have to go see Eric up at the real estate agency in Goult," John said one rainy morning. "Do you want to come? We could have a little lunch there—it will be good for you to get out." I had not been feeling well most days, so I hadn't been straying far from Gancel or the couch. On top of this, and what I am now sure was contributing to my physical state, was a deep sense of being uprooted. We had just made a massive transition, one that required separating from the kids, and I could feel my insides clinging to the one place that still connected me to them. Our history at Mas de Gancel was almost tangible, an umbilical cord that linked us to the day when we were together.

"I guess so," I mustered. Goult is a lovely historic village in the Luberon mountain range, a perfect hidden gem perched on top of a hill. While popular with tourists in the summertime, it is smaller than most of the other main villages—Gordes, Roussillon, and Bonnieux. We drove up the winding road with the rain drizzling and parked in front of the popular Café de la Poste. Eric's agency was on the corner overlooking the central square.

"Allo John et Lydia!" his eyes sparkled warmly as he spoke in rapid-fire French. John had been collaborating with Eric, who was listing the houses he had for sale through John's new Provence Life website. While the men chatted about their project, I passed the time flipping through the catalogue of Eric's house listings.

On the third page, I found myself gazing at a couple of old ruined buildings set in what seemed like a cluster of houses on the top of a little hill, surrounded by a vineyard and lavender fields. It was listed for what seemed like a very low price.

"Eric, c'est toujours a vendre cette ruine? (*Is this ruin still for sale?*)" I asked, after waiting for a polite moment to interrupt their discussion.

"It's in pretty bad shape, Lydia. I'm not sure it's what you and John are looking for."

"I've seen the listing," John said, nodding his head. "It's up on the hill overlooking Apt, which is a bit outside the sector we want to be in. It's a bit more rustic and rural over there. Plus, the only way to get to it is through the Col de Lourmarin," he added.

"The Col" is a long stretch of skinny road winding up the steep cliff hills between the popular villages of Lourmarin and Bonnieux. It was a treacherous climb with hairpin turns and cliff dropoffs that made the hair on the back of your neck stand up. At night, wild boar roamed the roads. In the summertime when the tourists arrived, driving through the Col was particularly frustrating as the traffic moved at a snail's pace as visitors gripped their steering wheels and pulled over to take pictures of the lavender fields below.

When we had begun our search for a house, John made three requests. He didn't want to have to drive through the Col on a regular basis, and he didn't want to do another massive renovation project. He wanted to dig into setting up his new real estate sales business, and he wasn't looking for massive drains on his time or energy. The last request might have seemed odd—he didn't love the smell of lavender. This might have had something to do with me breaking a bottle of imitation lavender all over the bathroom floor years before. Its fake, sickly stench permeated the house for weeks.

But I was drawn into this strange picture of the ruins; it had an enchanted, mystical feel to it. You could barely make out the stone walls through all of the vine growth that climbed them. And the sound of being in an area that was a bit more rustic and rural was music to my ears; I was one to color just a bit outside the lines.

"It's next to a lavender distillery," Eric continued. "It would be a big project, but I'll take you to see it if you wish."

John shot me a look of desperation as if to say, *You have to be joking me.* The property ticked all three of his "over my dead body" conditions.

"Yes, let's see it, Eric."

Two days later, we had agreed to rendezvous in the parking lot of the lavender distillery. John and I hadn't spoken about it much since being at the agency in Goult. I thought it best to leave a sleeping dog alone, yet felt a distinct tension in the air of the car as we wound our way delicately through the winding Col. Pulling into the driveway of the parking lot, I noticed a little blue sign: "Les Agnels."

Stepping out of the car, we couldn't help but take in the breathtaking views. Toward the north was a stunning rock face studded with trees, giving way to the clear blue expanse of the Provencal sky. Slightly to the west, you could see rows of cherry trees, one after the other, with the white cap of Mont Ventoux, the highest point in the region, peeking through. Then stretching across the entire spectrum were sweeping, open views of rolling vineyards and lavender fields with the Luberon Mountains in the distance.

"Holy shit," John said, taking in a huge breath as he scanned what lay before him. "Wow. This is something else. It's like I can see all of Provence right from here."

Eric arrived, stepped out of his car and immediately looked at our footwear. "Vous êtes bien chaussé? (*Are you wearing proper shoes?*)"

"Venez par ici (*Come this way*)," Eric said. He led us up a little incline, and before us stood a building, clearly very old. But it was difficult to even make out the shape of the structure as it was covered in vines, thick trunks of it, weaving their way into walls of stone.

"The Agnel family has been living in this hamlet and harvesting lavender for a very long time, hundreds of years. These buildings are very old, perhaps many families lived in them at one time. The place hasn't sold because of the state it is in. For starters, you can't quite make out what's inside this main building as it is half-collapsed and too dangerous to see inside."

We turned the corner and looked up unexpectedly to a beautiful facade of a house, with lovely stone window openings. It was surprising to find such a pretty side to the house, as the rest of the building was so demolished—this front part of it standing tall, yet only rubble was behind it.

We continued, making our way around the side of the building through tall weeds and what seemed like years of untended land. Turning the corner, we stopped to look down a rather steep incline. On the left-hand side was the old building we had just walked around; on the right side was another structure, a smaller house, almost invisible from the years of plant growth that had all but consumed it. I noticed a small wooden door, half-opened at the far end of the house. Pushing the door open, I scanned the large room. Ancient wood planks extended from one end of the room to the other. It was filled with an odd array of farming material—iron tools, wooden boxes, old tires. The planks looked too unstable to walk on, so I worked my way around the front of the house and entered into what felt like a foyer. From there I climbed a narrow staircase two floors up.

Old wasn't even the word for what was there. It was half-ruins, half-plants. The mixture of vines and stone gave the impression that it was literally alive. You could almost feel it breathing. I was instantly covered in goose bumps as I made my way back out of the small house and into the clearing. Standing in the center between the two buildings, I felt nestled, warmed, and grounded, as if I was tucked into the heart of the earth.

I stopped and turned to John. "This place is magical. It's so … I don't know. I don't even have words. I feel like I have already lived here." I waited for a pushback, a response that indicated I was crazy, but he looked back at me with his deep blue eyes, a small smile spreading across his face. He knew something powerful, something spiritual, was at work. I knew in that moment we were in sync, that he, too, trusted that the energy in the air had a life of its own.

Eric walked up to take in what we were saying. "Et alors?" he said, wondering what we thought of the rubbled mess.

"I have a sneaking suspicion that this is a done deal," John said, grinning as he looked over at me.

Before leaving the little house, I turned to look out of the small windowless frame. Out beyond I could see the rows of vineyard. To the right of them stood two rows of the biggest, most beautiful cherry trees I had ever seen. "John, look at this cherry grove. Can you believe it? Not one cherry tree, but rows of them. Not a speck of green could be found emerging from its deep gray branches—it wasn't the right season, but in my mind, I envisioned a sea of bright, white cherry flowers.

We didn't say much for what felt like a long time, Eric giving us each the space to take in the raw nature of what stood before us. It was almost too much to take in—the vast expanse of nature, the extent of its history, the footprint of time. We left knowing it was ours.

18

IDENTITY

*When you get uncomfortable in the place of the
unknown – that's where the magic happens.*

—Joe Dispenza

"WHAT THE HELL ARE YOU GUYS DOING?" I screeched as I watched Adrienne, Travis, and John all huddle around the freezer door in the kitchen at Gancel. They looked like they were up to no good as they attempted to stuff an item that was inside a black garbage bag into the freezer, laughing hysterically. "Lyd, she has termites, and we need to kill them!" Ade said emphatically.

The "she" being referred to was a two-foot-tall wooden carving of the Virgin Mary I had found on a recent trip to Guatemala. "We looked up how to get rid of termites in a wooden statue, and there were two options. One was to douse her in kerosene, and the other was to freeze her," Ade said flatly. "We knew you wouldn't be happy. And she needs to stay in there for two weeks."

I had stumbled on my Mary in an old shop in Antigua that was packed with dusty relics and old iron tools. I was struck by the look on her face—a beautiful combination of strength, compassion, and patience, like she would sit quietly, holding a safe and loving space for you forever, for an eternity. She was delicately carved, her features soft yet resilient. Under her left eye was a natural small line of darkened wood, as if a faint tear was falling from her eye.

Grace, I had thought. Perhaps this is what it looks like.

I consider myself spiritual, but don't hold any allegiance to any particular religion; to me they all seem to point to a common source. I have collected many items over the years that represent a connection to whatever source that is—Buddhas, Hindu figures, depictions of angels. My Mary, as I called her, had an incredibly calming effect on me, and I didn't hesitate in buying her.

"How the hell are we going to get that home to France?" John asked quizzically when I placed her two-foot-tall body upright on the floor at the hotel next to our suitcases. "I don't know—we'll figure it out!" We ended up leaving half of his clothes behind to make room for her in his case.

I watched as they pulled shelves and frozen vegetables out of the freezer to find a space big enough for her. It was lovely to be in the company of the people who knew me well, who didn't roll their eyes at strange mystical or spiritual habits, people who didn't question why I had lugged a massive wooden Virgin Mary halfway around the world. I was forever picking up white fluffy feathers if I saw them, tucking them into my pockets or placing them on our tables, sure they held messages in the moment. I read Tarot cards and had even completed a course as a certified reader. This spiritual side seemed to be expanding even more as time was progressing. I was now conversing with trees regularly alongside creating rituals and altars that I felt brought me closer to some sort of unknown source, a comforting universal heartbeat.

I propped myself up cross-legged on the kitchen countertop, a favorite perch in the house to have long chats about life. Emma sauntered in a few minutes later. She was on a fall break from college. Looking around the kitchen, I felt a wave of joy as it was full of people I loved.

"How do you feel things are going at GoPhil, Lyd? asked Travis. He had become increasingly involved at the foundation, slowly and skillfully taking projects off my shoulders, one by one. But somehow, I had been replacing them with new ones—there was so much to do and never enough time or people to get it all done.

"Yeah, let's have an update," Ade chimed in. I took a moment to think, taking a sip of my coffee. Strangely, I found myself bowled over by this simple question, and all of a sudden, I was filled with immense emotion, like a pot that was ready to boil over. It was as if everything that had happened in the past two years—the earthquake, the changes in me, the pain lodged inside my insides, the awakening, the trips, the meetings, moving in and out of Mas de Gancel, missing the kids—all rushed through me. With each passing day, I felt less able, less motivated, to forge on. And maybe, just maybe, life wasn't going to let me. As the words tumbled from my mouth, I struggled to keep the tears in. "I don't know if I can do this anymore. I can't seem to find the joy in it. I find it hard to open my computer in the morning," I cried.

I don't remember who suggested it, Travis or Adrienne, but

they both agreed wholeheartedly. I desperately needed time off, they said, to take a breath, to get perspective. But stepping away, even for a short period, was a foreign concept. Since giving birth to GoPhil Travel, I hadn't taken any real time off at all. I could be found on my computer working throughout the weekend and on holidays. I always traveled with my laptop on our vacations, stealing the morning hours while everyone slept to make sure I was on top of everything. But beyond all of this lurked an even bigger fear.

"Maybe I don't know who I am without it."

Since I was a little girl, I had sensed a great pull toward something, a profound longing of sorts, to be of use to the world. When I found the path to building GoPhil, I was thrilled to finally be acting upon it. For years I had lived with such an uncomfortable gap between what was happening out there in an incredibly unjust world, and me building my secure and comfortable life. For so long they had been two parallel realities that never seemed to cross. It had taken decades to take my first step to volunteer at the orphanage in Chennai, India, and then years to build what we believed to be a better, more effective way to channel a desire to help.

Working at GoPhil was like facilitating a Thanksgiving dinner every day—there was a place for people to gather, a place for different dishes they had lovingly brought from their homes and kitchens. Together we sat and shared, we communed together. All generations, cultures, and ethnicities, and it felt so right—like being part of a growing, caring global family. Now that I had found this place, I didn't want to let it go. I was scared to lose it. But at the same time, I couldn't take another bite of the meal, I just couldn't. I needed a pause to digest before I could go on. I had known this was part of the move back to France, but I hadn't gotten far in the work that needed to be done. It was too hard to let go.

Perhaps without me knowing it, this beautiful passion had slowly taken over my identity; it was a comfortable role. I had let it become *me*. It had recently dawned on me that I had four email addresses, and all of them had gophilanthropic in them. Not one of those addresses was in my own name. For a moment, I could see as clear as day that as much as it had been a meaningful project, GoPhil had also become my way of coping. I could escape whatever I couldn't handle in myself, while at the same time, know I was doing something good out there. It was the most perfect and acceptable place to take shelter, to hide from anything uncomfortable inside, even the pain that, despite all my efforts so far, still remained. And then there was the fact that nobody called me out on this coping mechanism. Working for the benefit of others was noble; it was altruism, for God's sake—what could be bad about that habit? At times I even felt put on a pedestal for it, and the fact that I didn't collect a paycheck for working all those hours earned me extra points.

It is often assumed that people who work in the charitable or giving sector must be really nice people, maybe even nicer than most. I can vouch that a great many certainly are, but I don't believe there's any more than in any other profession. "You must be an angel to do this work," I had heard over and over since building GoPhil. Of course, John and my close friends and family would snicker—*Jesus, if they only knew*. Personality traits were often associated with the job—immense patience, kindness, putting others before yourself. But I came with more.

Yes, something in the core of my being called me to do this work, but my imperfections didn't seem to slide into the puzzle neatly, and I felt ashamed of them. What would people think if they knew I swore and belched like a pirate, that I screamed at the kids so loud that at times the neighbors could hear, and that I loved trashy Netflix series (not going to even admit which ones) and eating cheese puffs? More importantly, what would they think of my weaknesses, my fear that I wasn't strong or courageous enough to get to the root of the issues we attempted to address, to ease the pain I knew on a cellular level existed out there.

Somewhere deep down, I longed to understand who existed inside of me before my formal role in building GoPhil began. What parts of my need to serve had to do with truly making things right, and what parts were born from the less bright, more shameful side of me? I had contemplated this a great deal over the years, in observing the way donors or volunteers behaved. At times I had been in awe of their incessant need to make a difference in the lives of others. It made me wonder whether we can be easily tempted to look over the fence and try and fix things on the other side, instead of tending to what needs attention on the inside.

I wondered whether it was something that already existed deep inside of me, or if it was something that was lacking, which drove my desire to want to help others. From a young age, I had been extremely sensitive, easily picking up on other people's emotions. At times I felt people's pain so acutely that I didn't know if it was my own. Raising Isabelle has been a clear example of this at work. It had been a complex journey, and one where I have had to literally hold my hands over my heart to try and stop the hurt that comes from inside. I am still navigating what part of that is hers and what is mine.

The more I worked with people and organizations who were facing the destructive effects of marginalization and human rights issues, the more pain I felt. This then drove my energy to fight back, to do something. In essence, it was both a blessing and a curse. This ability to sense deeply with others, one that I see often in my colleagues around the world, can help give you a force you didn't know you had in you, but it can also create blurred lines inside about what is yours to carry.

While my blinders had been removed two years prior, and I was listening in a new and beautiful way, I felt I couldn't get through a barrier. I considered all of this as I was nearing burnout, but didn't have the bandwidth to take it further. I simply couldn't catch my breath, couldn't tread the water anymore. I felt so tired of keeping it all together. Turning the mirror on myself, I considered whether this identity was blocking me from doing the inner work I needed, from exploring what it could be like to contribute from a place of whole and health, instead of an achy, empty tank.

I thought of the million reasons why I shouldn't take a break—*the team needs me, I have a responsibility, who else is going to do A, B, and C.* But it was Emma who saw things in clear light. "Mom, the way that I see it, GoPhil will survive your absence, they just will. It's your own guilt, your own fear that is getting in the way."

I distinctly remember the words coming out of her as she ate her cereal, as if it was plain as day to her. Guilt and fear. I might not have known the answer right then, but I knew she was right. I also knew what I had to do, and it felt like the riskiest, scariest, most selfish idea I had ever considered. There on that kitchen counter, I felt I had to finally release and let go. It was time to do me.

"You are right," I said, wiping my tears. "I need to stop. I need to see ... what's on the other side of this."

I struggled for days, trying to think of how I was going to admit to the team and the other two co-founders that I needed to walk away for a while, that I was burned out, that I felt as if I had been running and running for years. It wasn't a proud moment being in this spot—who wants to claim frailty or be forced to face and share our limitations? But looking back, I am now pretty sure that in these painful moments, we reclaim being human once again.

I decided on a three-month time frame, which I felt was long enough to feel the distance and get perspective, and short enough that I wouldn't lose the pulse of what was going on when I returned. And a secret part of me wanted to allow the space, the possibility that I didn't come back at all. I didn't know what I was going to encounter, who I would find, or what would speak to me during this time.

I knew that my absence would fall hard on the shoulders of others, and the timing could not have been worse as we were entering the most difficult period of the year when our fundraising efforts go full throttle. As expected, the news was a blow, an unforeseen shock to my teammates; it was not well-digested. I had to force myself to release the guilt and embrace what I was asking of myself. I knew I had a different job to do before I could continue anymore.

Travis, Ade, and Emma returned home, and Izzy and John resumed their respective lives. It felt strange to have the whole day in front of me, with no plan or purpose. My computer sat closed on my desk. I sat outside and looked out at the leaves turning red in the vineyard, letting the wind blow between my ears. Eventually, the leaves fell to the ground, and I decided to rake them. I raked for the better part of two weeks, feeling lost and confused inside, filling the big black bins, one after the other, methodically. But I loved the sensation of the fall air on my face and enjoyed watching the rays of sun cast light across the vineyard. The long days outside made me tired, and I began to have deep and restful sleeps, waking well after John had risen.

Looking around for other things to do, I noticed that we hadn't cut our massive row of lavender after their bloom that summer. I snipped all of them into neat round bushes, making a massive pile of lavender stalks. I couldn't fathom getting rid of all that sweet-smelling goodness. Sitting in the middle of the yard, I spent days pulling the dried flower heads off of their little brittle sticks, creating what became a very large, soft pile of dried flowers. Rummaging around the linen closet, I found an old throw pillowcase and filled it with the dried lavender. Pleased with myself, I propped up my new pillow on the couch in front of the fireplace, surprised at how the simplicity of these small tasks brought me such pleasure. Not only did it make the room smell nice, but it was also comforting to curl up with, especially during the long days when I didn't feel well enough to leave the couch. There were, I realized, other types of accomplishments, and they, too, could bring joy.

Some weekends we would make the drive with Izzy through the windy Col and wander around the vine-covered rocky ruins at Les Agnels, letting the world around us melt away into the rolling hills that looked over Apt and the clifftop villages of the Luberon Mountains. At times, we laid out big blankets and picnicked on *sandwiches jambon beurre*, nestled happily between the two crumbling structures. We sometimes wondered if we had been crazy to take the plunge in buying it. Seeing beyond its current state, a mess of fallen beams, stone, and overgrown roots, was on the one hand unimaginable, yet on the other, the most natural thing ever. With each minute we spent there, the vision of what it would become emerged as if it had always existed. I would climb into the car to return to Gancel, replete with something so safe and warm—like a child who had spent hours curled up in her mother's lap.

When I felt OK and had energy, I would walk the trails near our house, past Chateau Bas Winery and the Roman Ruins. With our dog Moe by my side, we would walk for hours, past groves of olive trees, grape vines, and old abandoned stone *cabanons*. I knew that a certain chapter had come to an end in my life and that I was on the threshold of discovering something new—something that had slowly, since the earthquake, been unfolding.

My mind reflected on all of the amazing people I had met in my last ten years of travel and foundation-building. I went through them all, one by one, in my mind, as if turning the pages of a scrapbook. I thought of Leng in Siem Reap, Cambodia, who, in the aftermath of destruction caused by the Khmer Rouge, had cared for abandoned children as if they were his own. There was Linda Hutchinson Burn, who had spent a life creating educational opportunities for at-risk Vietnamese girls. I saw the images of Lalitha on GB Road and of Pascal and Sharma as they fought on behalf of the rights of women and children in Delhi. There was Anuradha, who continuously risked her life saving children from a life of slave labor in Kolhapur. I carried on, to Julio and Maria Elena working at the clinic in Guatemala, Indra in Nepal, Hellen in Kenya. The list was very, very long, but I made it through each and every one, cherishing the memories I had of listening to them share their stories of hope and change in their villages and small offices.

Looking back, it came to me that they shared so many of the qualities that I admired—a delicate and powerful combination of courage, compassion, and perseverance, exhibited either through a hard battle of justice-seeking and advocacy or through gentle, devoted daily care. They had suffered in their own ways, yet perhaps they had found their strength and resilience, their greatest potential, from within this place. Maybe that place of pain had held some gifts. In observing their life's work from up close, I had been taught to never underestimate the potential that resides inside of us, should we have the courage to find it. Despite facing terrible challenges, they exemplified just how phenomenal the human being can be.

As I turned the corner on the path leading up to a cherry grove, my mind returned to one more person whose influence I was incredibly grateful for, whose spirit had resonated so acutely to me as a child that I felt she had spoken directly to my soul. It was Mother Teresa, in her steadfast and determined way, who had sparked the first flame, sounded the first call, that had opened my heart wider than I possibly thought it could open. All of a sudden, I stopped walking. Moe looked up at me confused, wondering what the problem was. Then the world went silent, and I had no choice but to stand and listen. *You need to give thanks before you can walk forward. You need to go back to the source.*

Years ago, I had been guided off the path that had us focused solely on our own security and achievements to one that had a much wider and more beautiful berth. This guidance had not come from me. It had been shared with me by people like Mother Teresa and all of the others who had come later in my life who had trusted and responded fully to what life had asked of them.

In that split second, I knew where I had to go and what I had to do. I ran fast and hard for the first time in a very long time, all the way back home. I ran straight to my desk and opened my computer, and booked a flight to Kolkata.

I had to be with her, I had to thank Mother Teresa, and properly. And maybe, just maybe, she might help me figure out what I was supposed to do next.

19

RUN AWAY

IN THE WEEKS LEADING UP TO MY TRIP, I continued to sort through all of the significant moments of my life so far, putting them into neat piles of happiness or pain so that I could later decide what to bring along with me in the next chapter. I felt like I was living in a gap, an empty space of unknowing, that was both necessary and terribly uncomfortable. Looking into the raging fire one evening at Gancel, I returned to a memory that I had been carrying with me for a long time, one that was somehow linked to my fierce desire to protect people in vulnerable situations, and yet one that carried with it a deep shame.

I was four years old, maybe five, living in Ottawa, Canada. My sister and I were both born there after our parents emigrated from England. Dad was a young and passionate physicist; Mum, a tender and lighthearted mother who worked as a real estate agent, yet if it were up to her, she would have been tending to plants full time in her garden with her girls at her feet. We had a small white house with a massive yard lined by gigantic looming willow trees. On long summer days, I would oftentimes meander over to the next door neighbor's house where my best friend Samantha lived with her older sister and her parents. We lived in a time when nothing was unsafe or abnormal about that type of freedom—kids could be gone for hours and nobody worried; mothers were happy to have a respite, knowing their children would eventually tumble through the door at dinnertime, dirty and hungry.

Spending time at Samantha's house was like traveling to another country. It smelled differently than mine and wasn't as tidy. Large rocks and minerals lined the bookshelves in their living room—the insides revealing an array of fantastic sparkling colors, rich purples and greens. Samantha's mom, who was kind and plump, could be found baking in the kitchen on most days. Something sweet and yummy was almost always in the white Tupperware that sat on their kitchen counter: a cake of some sort or a neat pile of peanut butter balls. My mother didn't make those.

But truth be told, I didn't like being at Samantha's house. Her dad walked around the house heavy-footed, wearing a sleeveless undershirt; he was missing almost all of his front teeth, and I swore I could hear him growl under his breath as he made his way around the house. Simply put, the man terrified me.

But outside to the left of the driveway facing the house, Sam had what nobody else in the neighborhood could compete with. As frightful as her dad might have been, he must have had his moments of brilliance, because one day, a dump truck pulled up to their house and delivered the biggest, most incredible pile of sand.

This wasn't a normal sand pit—it was more like a sand mountain that extended to the sky. It was the Mount Everest of sand piles, and we would spend hours and hours playing in it. We buried our bodies in it and drove toy cars and trucks all over it. Sand crept into our pockets, socks, and ears.

Being as scared of her dad as I was, I didn't like being inside the house much, so we spent almost all of our time together in the sand pit or riding our tricycles on the driveway. But there were days when we would be forced inside the red brick house, when it rained or on evenings when my parents might have gone out. Samantha and I would tuck ourselves into her bedroom and play with dolls on her bunk bed. On one occasion, I remember hiding my doll under one of her pillows. As I slid my hand underneath the pillow, I was surprised to feel something soft and light. Lifting the pillow up, I found strange little fuzzy clumps. Inching closer, I realized it was hair—Sam's hair. I remember being quite baffled in the moment, yet I don't recall either one of us reacting much to it. We were very young and there were lots of discoveries in a day that we didn't understand.

But over the following year or so, I began to notice growing bald spots on Sam's head, and my disdain for her father grew into knots in my stomach. On several occasions, I would wait until Samantha had turned her back or gone to the bathroom, and I would run home to the safety of my mum. I did it over and over, so many times, that one day Sam and her mother turned up at our house and rang the front doorbell.

"Why does Lydia run away?" her mother asked with what I knew was a heavy heart for her hurt child.

"Why does she leave Samantha out of the blue without any explanation?"

My mother begged and pleaded to get some sort of answer out of me, but nothing ever emerged from my mouth. I wanted to tell her Sam's house wasn't a safe place, that I knew something awfully wrong was going on over there, that I was somehow a part of it, but I didn't have the words. I would never have the words. I felt terrible for leaving her, for abandoning her—but something in my little body told me that kind of darkness wasn't something I had the power to protect myself from, nor fix.

Our family eventually moved houses—a few streets down and around the corner, then later across the border and into the US. Samantha and I lost touch, as naturally happens with childhood friendships. I saw her once in my late teens or early twenties. It had been an awkward visit—much had changed. Sam's mother had died of cancer, and her sister had passed away in a sudden, tragic avalanche. Sam was living with her dad, on and off, as she described it. She was also in and out of psychiatric hospitals. The bald spots on her head had disappeared, but I couldn't take my eyes off the scars that lined the length of her forearms and around her ankles. As we parted that day, I felt a terrible sadness creep into my body, and the familiar knot of shame and guilt reclaimed itself deep into my insides.

The memory fostered my sense of inadequacy in fighting the world's evil, and it fueled the ugly voices in my head that made me feel voiceless and insufficient—insignificant. I watched the flames in the fireplace die into red-hot embers. But what if part of it had also instilled in me the courage and passion to crawl around the world with a desire to help strengthen the work of brave people and programs who were standing up against this evil? My relationship with Samantha, and what might have gone on in that house, might have inspired me to fight back in a different way, at another time. Were these parts of us, the "cracks in our armor," blessings or curses?

These questions seemed to explain my desire to explore, to examine our need to give back. Could there be a distinction between what came from pure and genuine altruism, and the push that came from less bright, shadowy sources within ourselves? What if our desire to give back, in some cases, was because something had been taken from us in the first place, and it left a gaping, weeping hole? Were we to release these ugly experiences, as we are often told, and remove them like foreign toxins? Or did we need to incorporate, love, and nurture them as essential pieces of ourselves? Perhaps we need to accept and forgive our darker sides instead of constantly repressing them.

My gut was telling me that walking through our pain and owning it was, in fact, a path to find our greatness—but I still had a ways to go in truly believing it.

20

PILGRIMAGE

We're all just walking each other home.

—Ram Dass

LIGHT SOUNDS OF CRACKLING GRAVEL came from beneath the tires of the taxi making its way down the drive at Mas de Gancel. I shut the big wooden door behind me, pulling my small black carry-on behind me into the darkness. Twenty-some hours later, I walked into another dimension, out through the doors of the airport in Kolkata, formerly known as Calcutta, and into the warm, humid air. I took the biggest breath I could take, drinking in the smell of a place I had imagined since I was a young girl.

Palm trees lined the highway that, at this hour, was blissfully empty and serene. Finding a ticket booth, I prepaid a taxi to get to my guest house.

"Hello, I'm going to the Ivy House. Do you know where that is?" I asked, climbing into a well-worn cab. My driver, whose name I learned was Mohammed Akbar, nodded his head and motioned for me to get in. The car suddenly lunged forward, the gears grinding as if he had just learned to drive. I sat back and smiled, making myself comfortable. I had learned many years before to never assume a moment in India would go as you expected it to—I was sure it was partly what made the experience so rich. For me, India was a reminder that we don't have control in the way we think we do, and if we could allow space for that, India would give us gifts that we never could have imagined.

Mohammed and I chatted easily as he drove the car in an increasingly odd manner. He now seemed to want to avoid the gears altogether, the motor either straining as it revved too high or almost stalling as it slowed. Strangely, we had only shifted once since departing the airport. But my attention was more focused on what was outside my window, on the stunning yet deteriorating colonial structures and the sea of housing made from makeshift materials, tarps, and tin sheeting that bordered the roads. Families were just beginning to wake and start their morning fires.

Forty-five minutes later, we pulled into a quiet, tree-lined road off one of the city's main thoroughfares. I was relieved as I noticed a small, discreet sign labeled "Ivy House" tucked in front of a tree. "That's it, Mohammed, we are here," I said, thankful for the somewhat uncomfortable ride, but happy to have been safely delivered. Traveling to so many faraway places, at all hours of the day or night and oftentimes alone, I have developed a certain sixth sense for placing trust in people. It has been an essential tool in navigating the unknown on the road. These brief encounters, like the one with

Mohammed, might be short-lived, but strung together, I always found they interconnected; they told a story. We smiled at each other and wished one another good luck in life, knowing we would most likely never see each other again.

Wanting a quiet, local experience, I had chosen a small, family-run guest house. Peering through the locked gate down the driveway, all seemed deserted at this early hour. I was surprised as a shirtless man, whom I deduced to be a nightwatchman, suddenly appeared from a tiny security office next to the gate. He approached me, a bit disheveled, pants twisted around his waist. I sensed mild frustration as he mumbled something to me in Bengali while opening the gate for me to enter.

I followed him down a small red-brick path to a narrow staircase and up one floor. Undoing an old padlock and handing me the oversized key, the man turned and left as abruptly as he had arrived, back to bed, I assumed. The main building of the guest house had been full for my first night, so they had booked me in the owner's private house. Sitting on the bed, I took a look around—feeling as if I had walked into someone else's life. The room was small and clean, the walls covered in family pictures. Trinkets of all sorts and books lined the shelves.

I awoke two hours later with the hot sun searing my cheek and loud banging noises coming from the small courtyard outside my window. After taking a much-needed shower, I wandered down to a small wooden room that opened up to the outdoor patio. Staff were milling around happily, serving a table of guests and arranging a small breakfast buffet table. I noticed the night guard's face immediately. He had transformed, now wearing round-rimmed glasses and a crisp, button-down shirt. "Good morning, ma'am!" he said, beaming with a wide and beautiful grin.

Ivy House was a cozy and inviting place, the courtyard dripping with plants and flowers, and a clean, lightness of energy was in the air. I was pleased with myself for having spent the extra effort to find a special place. I sat for some time, sipping tea and nibbling on toast as I considered the day ahead of me. Knowing that I would be tired from the journey, I had only one objective for the next few hours, and that was to make my way to the Mother House of the Missionaries of Charity. The Mother House was both the resting place of Mother Teresa and home to the organization's headquarters that now had 4,500 nuns actively working in more than 600 missions across 133 countries. It was known as the heart and soul of the organization. In the afternoon, I wanted to attend the weekly orientation offered to anyone who wished to volunteer their time at any of the Missionaries of Charity houses. There were nineteen of them in all across Kolkata alone, each with a unique focus to serve different populations in need. There were homes for at-risk women, children with disabilities, and the dying. There was an AIDS home and a nursing home, a school for street children, and a home that cared for people suffering from leprosy.

Due to my extensive reading about Mother Teresa and the Missionaries of Charity, better known as the M.C., I was no stranger to the controversies surrounding some of their practices. Since founding the organization in 1950, Mother Teresa and the M.C. had been accused of everything from using unsafe or outdated medical practices, to baptizing dying patients. Questions surrounded some of the high-profile yet potentially fraudulent funding that was accepted through the organization. Some accused Mother Teresa of not addressing the root causes of poverty, focusing too much on the symptoms. Over the years, I had made room in my mind for some or all of these allegations to be true—for who amongst us can claim perfection? I felt there was a larger picture with a much bigger meaning and message to be learned from her life's work. It had to do with offering love, compassion, and dignity, no matter what circumstances a human being found themself in. She believed in the power of small actions, of humility, and being a part of what needed to be done. *Do not wait for leaders; do it alone, person to person.* All of this resonated with me on every level.

But this aside, I did have some personal issues when it came to the values surrounding short-term volunteering—how it could be self-serving to the person wanting a "do-good" experience. Spending a week or two at one of her missions could no doubt fall into this category. Given GoPhil's advocacy against the risks of unskilled short-term volunteering, I couldn't deny that from the outside, my stay could be judged similarly. But I knew where I stood in my heart. My personal intention was to be in the presence of Mother Teresa's spirit, in the place where she had been inspired to devote her life and her soul to caring for others. I would offer any simple labor needed during that time, in any way that was needed. I wasn't offering this as a donation of time, but out of deep gratitude for what she had built and for the people she served.

A butterfly-like feeling swept through my stomach, bringing with it a mixture of excitement and nerves at the thought of simply being there. I collected my things from my room and made my way in an Uber to A.J.C. Bose Road, located in one of the poorest areas of the city. When I arrived, I was surprised at how discreet it was—the building was rather small for such an important site. If it weren't for the two nuns dressed in their traditional white-and-blue cotton saris walking through the door, I would have easily walked by without ever noticing.

I entered the main door and walked into the small courtyard. A handful of visitors were walking around alongside missionaries, who seemed to be going about their daily tasks. I climbed the stairwell that led to an austere little bedroom, where Mother Teresa had lived and worked from the 1950s through to her death in 1997. It reminded me of visiting the Gandhi Smriti in New Delhi. While it was the site of Mahatma Gandhi's brutal assassination, it also housed a little room where he spent his last days, where he spun his cotton, wrote and slept. Both rooms were as bare bones as it comes, but there was a beauty in the raw simplicity. Maybe with less, they could see more.

I moved on from Mother Teresa's bedroom and made my way to another room that served as a museum, displaying some of her personal belongings—her crucifix, sandals, and dinner bowl. Next to the museum was a larger room, and in the middle stood her marble tomb. My heart skipped a beat as I glanced in, but a crowd of visitors passed by me abruptly, suddenly filling the room. Not wanting to join them, I took a few steps back.

I found a wooden bench in the courtyard. I sat and closed my eyes, listening to the soft sounds of nuns chanting their midday prayers. There was a peacefulness to the house—it was busy, but deeply serene at the same time. She might have passed to another realm, but her presence seemed to fill every corner of the building.

A light breeze swept through the courtyard and, opening my eyes, I saw a small white feather land on the bench beside me. Relief washed over me, and I couldn't help but feel immense privilege for being there, like the awe you feel in a cathedral or mosque, where time and the world outside are replaced by something else, something sacred. *Thank you, Teresa. Thank you for all that you offered of yourself. In doing so, you have shown us what we can be.*

At some point, it was time for all of the visitors to leave—the building closed in the middle of the day so the sisters could regroup privately. I now had three hours to kill in a not-so-great part of town before the orientation session that afternoon. I considered finding a place to eat, but I wasn't hungry. I was hot and feeling jet-lagged. Wandering out into the road, I noticed the sign for the Mother House on the side of the building. I stopped to take a selfie, struggling a bit with the angle. A volunteer that had come from inside the building noticed me. "There's a nice spot for a picture from over this way," she stated confidently. Handing her my phone, I followed her while she took the time to line things up perfectly, as though she knew firsthand how precious the moment was, like she had been there herself.

"Hi, I'm Agatha Chai. I'm headed to New Market if you want to join me. Are you planning on volunteering? If so, I'll show you where the meeting will be held—it's in a building not far from here. We pass it as we go." I recognized New Market from my reading of the city's main sites, famous for selling everything from spices to clothes and electronics.

I'm not even sure I answered her but simply took her direction and followed, like a child in a kindergarten class. We needed to walk in single file as the sidewalk was packed with people and vendors. I strained to keep up with her; she had a fast pace, weaving in and out of the crowd easily. I tried to guess her age; she had the energy of a sixteen-year-old, yet I noticed some gray hairs coming from her loose ponytail tied at the nape of her neck. I was struck by the way she took her steps—they were surefooted and determined, yet light. For a moment, I marveled at how some people's spirits could be so evident, so immediately.

Turning every so often, she spoke to me freely, with a smile that never left her face. Agatha explained her background while we strode, at the same time pointing out various landmarks along the way. I was surprised when she shared that she was a domestic laborer in Malaysia. Based on the way she held herself, I had presumed that she held a more prestigious position. And wasn't that an unfortunate assumption to make.

"How long are you here for?" I asked, trying to catch up to her. "For a month—it's my fifth time. I just keep coming back," she said happily.

At the market, she bade me farewell, reminding me of the way back. I saw her later that afternoon at the meeting, where she gracefully commanded a room of thirty or so new volunteers, arranging for us each to sit privately with an M.C., explaining why we were here, what skills we had, and how long we planned on staying. Afterward, the sisters would match us with a mission location, giving us the times we were to show up. We were each sent away with a small plastic medallion of the Virgin Mary, hung from a simple brown piece of string.

The meeting ended, and it was a shock to go from the

tranquility of the room to the mayhem of the busy streets outside. It had felt like an endlessly long day, and I was numb from exhaustion, both physical and mental, as I left the building. I pulled out my phone to arrange an Uber, only to notice that my phone was desperately low on batteries. It didn't help that thirty minutes later I was in the same spot, after three missed attempts at meeting the driver—it was impossible to find each other in the throngs of people and rush hour traffic. I began to worry, not badly, but enough to get my blood moving, as I realized I didn't really know where I was. I was in a part of town where few tourists ventured, and little English was spoken. As my phone died, I began to stress about how I would find my way.

Suddenly a car pulled over, and a man rolled down the window to stick his head out. "American woman, this woman, same lady, same lady!" he screeched. I was amazed and relieved to see Mohammed Akbar. I climbed into his taxi, and we lunged forward into traffic, the gears grinding as we went. We were both laughing loudly, stunned at the serendipity of the chance meeting and acting like two long-lost friends who had been reunited. "Two time one day same lady," he must have said at least ten times as he drove me back to the Ivy House. "Fifteen million people in Kolkata and same lady two times one day!" he continued. I was well aware that the price he had charged me that morning was a foreigner price—probably ten times a local fare, so he was most likely overjoyed at his luck of landing this more than once. But I, too, felt fortunate at having been so lucky. I fell asleep that night with a warm feeling inside, a knowing that life was not at all what we saw from its surface. I sensed that it was perfectly and magically rigged behind the scenes, that our connections and encounters were less haphazard than we would like to believe. If we could replace some of the fear we carry each day with trust that it is all as it should be, we might have more space to focus on more important things.

My alarm went off at 5 a.m. We were to meet back at the Mother House before heading off into our various locations. I was thrilled to have been placed at Nirmal Hriday, formerly Mother Teresa's Kalighat Home for the Sick and Dying, the first of all the homes she established in her lifetime. Before she sought permission to use it, the building was an old Hindu temple to the goddess Kali, the Hindu goddess of time and change. In 1952, it became the first hospice to care for people who were dying, abandoned on the city's streets.

I arrived on time and headed downstairs with the other volunteers to have a light breakfast of tea, sliced white bread, and bananas. In the walk down, I heard several languages being spoken—French, Spanish, Japanese, Italian, English. Despite the spread of nationalities, there was a distinct sense of unity amongst us. There didn't seem to be ladders of success in the room; our time over the next days would reveal how little that mattered. As we nibbled on breakfast, each of us shared why we had come.

"She inspired me."

"I just needed to come."

"I came once and had to come back."

I connected immediately with a man named Gerald, who appeared to be in his sixties. I had been captivated by his beautiful smile and crisp blue eyes. Our idle chitchat moved quickly to the story behind him being there. He had come to the M.C. and been matched with the Titagarh mission that worked with the community of lepers, run by a group of brothers as opposed to sisters. Over time, they taught him everything they knew about how to treat the wounds of the leper community. Gerald was a quick study and also displayed an innate sense and ease in treating people who were looked upon by most as repulsive members of society. The brothers had asked Gerald to stay on for longer.

He described how he left his life in France for a life on the streets in Kolkata, treating whomever needed attention. It had been twenty years, and he still continued to walk up and down the city's grim back alleys offering basic health treatment. It made me think of Hermano Pedro in Antigua, Guatemala. He, too, had been a missionary. I immediately thought of my own judgment toward missionaries, feeling that they were oftentimes giving services in an attempt to convert people to their belief systems. I had been adamant in my thoughts about this over the years, which had been fueled by all of the faith-based charities whom I had watched usurp control over communities by dangling funding in front of people in situations of desperation. But in listening to Gerald, I sensed there might be room for another side to that story. Perhaps in some cases, like his, and that of Mother Teresa and Hermano Pedro, it was their devotion that gave them the trust to be able to give so fully.

Gerald glowed as he spoke, describing each day as an immense blessing. Amongst wounds and open sewered lanes, he had found and exchanged joy in a setting most people feared.

"Life chose a path for me. I simply responded," he said. The words struck me hard as we were being called by groups to make our way to our mission locations.

Gerald turned to me as we headed up the stairway, and asked, "How long will you stay?"

"Only a few days," I said shyly, humbled by the decades he had spent here. Then I remembered Mother Teresa's message—*It is within the smallest acts that we feel the greatest joy.* I wasn't going to allow myself to measure my efforts or judge my impact. I just wanted to be there, to be present and open for the experience that was meant for me.

A small handful of other volunteers were also assigned to Nirmal Hriday. We followed two M.C.s out into the busy streets, walking in the wake of their flowing cotton saris. We rode the public bus for twenty minutes, then walked another ten minutes nearing the Kalighat Kali Temple, passing rows of devotees and vendors selling flowers and incense as we went. Families who were living on the streets were busy making breakfast over open fires, some children still peacefully fast asleep, lost in their dreams.

At the end of the road stood the Nirmal Hriday, a tallish white stone building that used to be a site where pilgrims stayed while visiting the temple. Despite its chipped and dirt-covered facade, it claimed a certain elegance. Mother Teresa had discovered the streets to be full of people, many of whom were in the late stages of tuberculosis, dying without any care whatsoever. She rallied the municipality to give her the pilgrims' building to care for them, which they did, and to this day it offers free hospice for men and women who are sick or dying without anyone to care for them.

An older M.C. greeted us at the door and led us into the main hall. I was quickly ushered into the side that housed the women. I stopped to take in the scene of the long room lined with tidy beds.

The room was familiar to me—I had seen many photographs of it over the years. It smelled fresh, and soft light cast rays across a newly mopped floor. I noticed about twenty women, mostly older, grouped at the end of the room where they were being fed lunch. Some seemed able to feed themselves, many were not and were being helped by either staff or volunteers. We walked by them into the central rooms where the food was cooked, dishes washed, and where large concrete vats of water were used in a distribution line for hand-washing clothes. There must have been two dozen people, a mixture of staff and volunteers, working hard. Water was splashing on the floor and dishes were passed from one person to the other, some dishes heaped with food, others ready to be cleaned. But like I had found with the Mother House, amongst the intense busyness, there was also a serenity, a peacefulness to the chaos.

"Come upstairs first," an M.C. directed us. We were led up a staircase and given aprons to wear and small lockers to store our things.

I don't recall any meeting or instructions on what to do. I was led to the central washing area where I was simply sucked into a sea of hot, soapy water, dishes, and hands. I joined the group that was washing clothes, mountains and mountains of them, pajamas and sheets and pants and pillowcases. I watched as a group moved in sync, plunging the dirty clothes in one vat, rinsing in another, then moving them to a small machine that spun them for a few minutes. From here they were dumped into a plastic bowl to be taken upstairs to line dry. Like me, my fellow volunteers found a space or hole in the work line, and before any one of us could ask a question, we, too, were in the flow.

A man handed me a plastic tub of clean clothes and motioned for me to follow the person in front of me who was taking a similar tub up two flights of stairs to the rooftop. Resting it on my hip, I was shocked at its weight and struggled to get a good grip. When I finally did, I climbed the first of hundreds of stairs I would climb that day, straining with the sheer weight. I was pleased when I reached the top, yet intimidated at my level of exhaustion after only ten minutes of work. Looking up, the entire terrace was covered in washing lines, and rows of pajamas and sheets billowed in the soft, hot breeze. Beyond it was Kolkata's endless city skyline. I set the tub down and happily began to hang the clothes, notably worn and torn in places, but clean and fresh.

It took a handful of hours for ten of us to hang all of the wash, which would then be folded and brought back down later that day. The following morning, the same routine would take place. When we weren't washing clothes, we were doing dishes or helping with the lunch service, feeding those who couldn't lift their arms. There were staff members who didn't seem to be official M.C. as they were not wearing saris, yet they must have had authority; they commanded with firm and loving orders to us and one another. At times, we were told to assist in taking women to the bathroom. Many could no longer walk, so we were shown how to drag them on red plastic chairs, at times pulling them behind us and at others, pushing the chairs in front of us into the toilet areas where more-trained staff were there to help them privately.

The volunteers were given the jobs that required the least amount of direction, skill, or experience. They entailed mostly labor—bathroom chair-dragging duty, dishes, and laundry. The hours and days slipped by naturally, and while the work was physically hard, it was a joy to just be a part of a system. There wasn't a lot of chat between us; it seemed like everyone, including me, was content to be quiet and useful. Our jobs, backgrounds, and home lives existed in another place, in another time. I don't even recall sharing our names. We just worked together, side by side, hour by hour, doing what needed to be done, together as a whole.

It reminded me of the concept of karma yoga, or "yoga of action" that is spoken about in the ancient Hindu text, the Bhagavad Gita. In karma yoga, there is work, but no attachment to the result or what you will receive for it. In this sense, the action is a form of prayer. That's what it felt like to be at Nirmal Hriday. We knew we were there to care for others, but the focus was not on making a difference. It was more about the simplicity of just being a part of something that cared for all—and we were included in that. There was something deeply comforting and uncomplicated about it. Like a plant that was growing, without effort. Thought wasn't necessary—just presence and openness and activity.

At times, we were encouraged to sit with the patients, to throw balls or sing or massage stiff muscles. You could tell there were deep relationships between the M.C., staff, and patients. Our presence as volunteers in these more intimate moments was appreciated, but it was extra, not altogether essential, and this felt appropriate. I noticed right away that it wasn't just the volunteers who wore the Mary Medallion, but all who were living at Nirmal Hriday. While the organization was rooted in the Catholic faith, it didn't feel defined by it. To me, the medallion represented a spirit that transcended any one defined faith—Mary's image seemed to gracefully

LIGHT THROUGH THE CRACKS

capture surrendering to the moment and offering yourself to what that moment was asking of you. Strangely, that's exactly what it felt like to be there.

One day I was surprised to see a woman who was brought in from the streets on a stretcher and gently placed onto a bed in the women's dormitory. I was pushing a patient to the bathroom and needed to pass directly by the woman's bedside. Her face was skeletal, the thinnest layer of flesh stretching over bones. Her eyes were sunken and vacant, and she was lying on her side, wrapped in cotton cloth. Part of her right side was exposed, and I could see sores all over. Her hip bone was showing through the skin. My heart dropped into my stomach as I passed her, thinking there was no way she would live through the day.

Later that afternoon, after a doctor had examined her and tended to her wounds, an M.C. approached me, pushing a bowl of mashed lentils into my hands and directing me to feed her. I looked over my shoulder, thinking surely, they needed someone more qualified than me. Before I could respond, the M.C. had turned and walked away, leaving me standing there between the rows of beds. I walked over to the woman's bedside and sat by her, conscious that I couldn't even speak to her in her language. She had been resting but must have sensed my presence, and opened her eyes. I motioned to the bowl, indicating that I would be helping her to eat. I was pleased when she opened her mouth—*yes, you need food*, I could hear myself say. I continued to speak to her softly as she took tiny mouthfuls of the soft lentils. When she no longer opened her mouth, I stopped. She turned, and we looked long and deep into each other's eyes. There was no need for language—my heart opened and from it flowed something that I knew came from far beyond my physical frame. Her eyes shined big and beautifully, radiating back, filling me with a warm glow. We touched each other's hands, and I left her to rest.

When I wasn't at Kalighat, I spent my time wandering the streets of Kolkata. I walked until I couldn't walk anymore or until the sun slipped away behind the dusty horizon. I thought of the woman who had been brought into the center and wondered whether she was still alive. I tried to imagine what had gone through her mind as she suffered on the streets, alone, while people walked by her. How was it that we could do this to one another? What kind of fortresses have we built around our hearts to be able to step over people in need? What mattered more than caring for each other—for our parents, children, friends, lovers, husbands, and strangers on the street? Our money, success, and material things—so much of what consumed our time, could never compare, yet the world had designed itself to magnify anything but this truth. It's our togetherness that forms the basis for meaning in life. How have we forgotten this?

I remembered having read *The City of Joy* by Dominique Lapierre, who had described Kolkata and life in the slums as teeming with sickness, sewers, and leprosy, yet somehow brought into light the joy that comes from our human connection. When I had read this book back in my thirties, well before GoPhil, I had been deeply scared of what I might find in such a place, but I also knew the answers to life were there too. Answers to what, I didn't know yet, but I was sure it had to do with the light and the magic, the love that we can only feel when we come together, when we turn toward, acknowledge, and tend to each other.

I thought about a strange encounter I had had that morning when I entered the main hallway. A sister had approached me with a big, warm smile on her face—it was as if she had been waiting for me. "Hello," she said, taking my hand. She began to ask me questions about my life, and in a matter of minutes, I felt she knew all of it. Afterward, she took my arm and stroked it gently. "You are weak, my dear. You need to strengthen yourself. This work is heavy and you need stamina." Her words were kind, but they were also a warning that I couldn't continue to carry the weight of the world like a physical tub of laundry on my hip. Like Arun Gandhi had also taught me, there was a lighter, more joyful, and more powerful way forward.

I ached as I took each step, wondering how Mother Teresa could endure witnessing both the poverty on the streets but also the poverty inside all of us that allowed it to happen each and every day. In *Come Be My Light: The Private Writings of the Saint of Calcutta*, it is exposed that while she was an icon for care, little was known of the deep well of desolation that she endured for decades in her inner world. In her private notes, she admitted, "If I ever become a Saint—I will surely be one of darkness. I will continually be absent from Heaven—to light the light of those in darkness on earth."

The author of that book, Brian Kolodiejchuk, spoke of how she knew how to suffer, but she also knew how to laugh. How had she forged on in such a seemingly effortless and extraordinary way while carrying this internal suffering within her was a mystery to me. And still, where did she get her stamina? I needed to know. Then I thought of the beautiful, effortless energy that had flowed through my body in Nirmal Hriday. It hadn't come from me, yet it had flowed through me with a force and strength that couldn't overcome anything. Maybe this is what sustained her, giving her the ability to carry out all that was asked of her. I had a hunch that Agatha and Gerald knew and were drawing from this same energy, alongside all of the other formidable people I had met in building GoPhilanthropic. If so, then perhaps we all had access to it, should we be willing to search for it through the pain, instead of running from it or dragging it with us. Perhaps there was a way to tap into this current of love and compassion, and maybe, just maybe, it had no end. It wasn't the size of the tank that held a limited amount of fuel that mattered, but access to the infinite source that was the key.

Thank you, Teresa, thank you, Agatha and Gerald. Thank you, Kolkata. Thank you for showing me it's all here. We have everything we need inside of us and between us.

The Mary Medallion hung steadily over my heart on its little brown string as I walked back to the Ivy House. And for the first time in a while, maybe forever, I began to feel the strength in my own step. I knew I could trust in the path, and in the ground underneath my feet.

21

NOURISH

ON THE LAST LEG OF THAT TRIP TO INDIA, I hadn't gone home directly. I had carried on to Kolhapur in Maharashtra to visit our longtime partner Anuradha Bhosale, director of AVANI, an organization leading the way in child rights and women's empowerment.

I had met Anuradha Bhosale in 2007 through Arun Gandhi, who had been involved in her work for some time. She was fearlessly setting the stage without much of the world around her knowing, deconstructing the complex forces that surrounded child labor in India. Our single question to her under the hot sun all those years ago had been: "What can we do to help you?" Anuradha's answer came quickly: "A cell phone and a tuk-tuk." And with this small, eight hundred dollar seed investment, she made the rounds to every surrounding village in her radius made up of under-resourced migrant populations, informing them of their human rights and inspiring them to fight on behalf of themselves.

Anuradha was addressing the issue of child labor through accountability and empowerment, forcing both law enforcement and factory workers alike to uphold the constitution that forbade forced labor. She encouraged parents to use education as a means for their children to escape a cycle of poverty instead of following in their bonded footsteps.

She was painstakingly hunting for the root of deep social inequities, mobilizing every strata of society, including local businesses and the media, to play an active role in making life more just for all. The results of her community engagement have continued to reveal themselves, with over half of her programs now being handed over to local government agencies. People from "Dalit" or "untouchable" communities are now recognized members and contributors of society, and their children are attending schools. Through AVANI-supported self-help groups, women are uplifting and supporting one another, advocating for their own rights, gaining micro-loans and saving money to launch small businesses and group enterprises.

Over the course of a decade, we would see the power of community engagement at work before our eyes, and we would learn how partnerships can play a critical role in expanding impact. Widespread forced child labor in the Kolhapur region has all but ended due to her efforts.

But what has been most poignant about her life's work is that she believed in the importance of what people can do for themselves. Handouts and charity have never been words in her lexicon. Even people who are not yet aware of their own human rights deserve to know and act from their own potential.

Anuradha and I had forged a deep friendship over the years, our conversations often straying from her work as an activist and mine around the foundation's support for her projects. In our intimate moments together, we snuck in questions about life, our children, and our love for gardening. We spoke about menopause, the importance of weaving in enough time for morning walks and yoga stretches, and the difficulties with grant applications that so often didn't bear fruit. Over the course of our years working together, it was becoming clear that we now needed each other in ways that went far beyond work. We promised to stand by one another as women, mothers, and nonprofit builders, through the good days and the not-so-bright ones.

It had been two years since we last saw each other. We hugged one another tightly in the lobby of the hotel, then found a quiet place to sit and catch up over tea. She brought me up to speed on all that was happening. AVANI was providing education to over three thousand children who migrated to the region every summer to work in the brick kilns, and she was in the process of conducting an intensive survey to track and ensure that they continued to attend school when they returned home and that their local schools accepted them. They had also recently launched a progressive waste composting center, run by women who had formerly been working in dangerous conditions as waste pickers, with no access to health care or education for their children. AVANI had developed a program whereby the women collected wet waste from houses and then created fertilizer that was sold to local farmers.

"Lydia, I want to expand this to cover the whole city, but we need a much bigger composting machine for this. It is an important project for environmental protection. They are cleaning up the city yet also providing income for women who otherwise cannot get proper employment," she explained passionately.

The timing of my visit was perfect, as I was able to join the tail end of GoPhil's Journey to India—they were finishing up in Kolhapur and meeting with Anuradha at the same time. It was strange for me not to be guiding that trip as I had always done. Amy Leonard, a volunteer and ambassador from Denver, was leading the journey; I was thrilled to see others taking on the role, bringing with them new and fresh energy.

I joined as the group visited the brickyards where children used to be working for grueling hours a day, but now, thanks to AVANI's efforts, spent their days learning in small makeshift classrooms run by passionate teachers. I sat back and observed how Anuradha and the staff at AVANI brought to life the intricate variables at play that related to bonded labor, gender inequity, and the need for communities to be a part of their own advocacy.

As our group listened fully, you could almost feel their perspectives opening up as they gently asked questions, expanding their understanding of the realities, seeing in a way they couldn't have seen from the other side of the world. I thought back to the moment in my kitchen in Provence where I had wondered about my ability to continue. Now sitting in this tiny classroom facing joyful children who were building a future with what they deserved, there was no need to question anything.

One afternoon, Anuradha brought me to a small piece of land that, years before, Arun Gandhi had donated to her efforts. They had wanted to build a school on it in memory of Arun's wife

Sunanda, but the shape and size of the plot were not conducive. Instead, they built a small, simple dome that Arun stayed in when he visited. Anuradha admitted to using it often as a retreat—a place where she could hear the wind blow, where she could take a small respite from being on call, day and night, by women and children in crisis situations.

I walked behind her as she strode peacefully onto the grounds, a big happy grin spreading across her face as she showed me the way, pointing to various fruit trees she had planted. The environment was surreal, juxtaposed against the harsh conditions that the migrant families she worked with faced in their cramped villages. Here we were surrounded by lush green hills and flowering bougainvillea. The air smelled fresh. The dome was cool inside, and she ushered me onto the bed that was placed in the middle of the room.

"Here, rest ... I'll make some tea." When she returned, she shared that she had struggled with finding a home, that the years of fighting for human rights and advocating had been difficult—there had been many sacrifices along the way. She was raising two children of her own while putting her life at risk for others. What little money she had to support herself, she almost always put back into her programs, forcing her to regularly move in and out of small, rented apartments. On many nights, she slept on the floor with the women at the night shelter she had established.

She now came to the dome to breathe and to give to herself, something she had rarely done in her earlier years. For years, I had seen her suffer physically from the terribly long hours and grueling workload she endured, let alone the stress of the situations she dealt with. I had never seen her at ease before, and it was a beautiful sight to see her finding joy in what was around her. While she spoke passionately of what she had yet to do, she also seemed content with what she had already accomplished. Home, she explained, for the moment, was found here in the serenity of the dome, amongst her flowering trees, the roaming buffalo, and a pack of rescued dogs that she loved to bits. I knew in that moment there was something to learn from it.

As we readied to return back to the city, Anuradha peeled a banana, offering me one. "Here, eat," she said, holding out a piece.

"No, I can't—I'm not allowed to have fruit." We had had long chats over the past months. I had told her about not feeling well but that I was following a Chinese medicinal routine that I was sure would bring results.

Anuradha didn't hold back.

"Well, it's not working. You look shriveled," she said disapprovingly. She reached out and pinched my face, then squeezed my upper arm as if I were one of her own children. "You need to see Dr. Haldvedekar. He's an Ayurvedic practitioner and healer. I'll make an appointment with him for tomorrow," she said firmly, not asking my approval.

My meeting wouldn't be the last that I would have with Dr Haldvedekar over the next two years. The depth of Ayurveda, what is known to be the oldest historically recorded traditional medicine, would take time to reveal itself to me. Ayurveda is translated as "knowledge of life," and while it is rooted in treating illnesses with nature-based, herbal medicines, the fundamentals stretch far beyond human physiology. Its healing involves a balance and harmony between our physical constitution, emotional nature, and spiritual outlook. All of these are thought to be interconnected with similar forces within the universe, which is composed of five elements: air, water, space, fire, and earth. These five elements form the three basic biological energies called doshas, and they control the basic physiological functions of the body. When they are out of balance, sicknesses and ailments occur.

Anuradha picked me up early in the morning for our visit, before GoPhil's program for the day got underway. Like Dr. Chi, the examination took all of four minutes. He felt my pulse for two seconds, pushed his hands into my abdomen, sending me into fits of pain, then handed me a bag with hundreds of neatly folded paper packets of herbs that had been packaged by his wife in his own kitchen. He agreed with what Dr. Chi had said—I lacked fire power, my circulation was not good and, as a result, my stomach was not digesting food well. This was causing a host of imbalances across my organs.

"You need to eat soft, warm, and nourishing foods, nothing raw, dry, or harsh. And don't skip meals. Take your herbs regularly, and your pain should be gone in about six months. Come back and see me then," he said matter-of-factly.

He hadn't explained much about Ayurveda in that meeting. I would learn much more in future visits, including the importance of incorporating meditation and yoga into the healing practices to restore balance to the system. In that moment, the simplicity of the terms "warm and nourishing" were what resonated loudly, and I knew them to be significant.

Perhaps this was what had been missing for me in the approach I had taken with the Chinese diet—it had reinforced a pattern of harsh denial and sacrifice that had already gone on too long.

Walking out of Dr. Haldvedekar's office, I could hear the words of Evelina in Costa Rica ringing in my ears—"Nurture yourself. You need to heal. It is going to take some time." It certainly had taken time, what had felt like an endlessly long time, but slowly their meanings were finally weaving themselves together into a beautiful, bright image. I was realizing that giving to myself, as I had been doing for so many others for so long, was an indispensable, valuable, and fundamental part of healing myself. It wasn't the selfish act I had thought it to be. It was, in fact, the ultimate expression of gratitude for all that we are.

The concept of going in and truly listening deep within myself to honor what my physical body needed, as well as what my soul craved, was a critical turning point. I realized that in ignoring and holding out on my own needs, I had not been honoring this most incredible gift. And that gift was recognizing my own beauty, what I had to offer the world.

"Now let's go get breakfast," Anuradha said excitedly, grabbing my arm. She guided me to a simple local restaurant on the corner of the street near the doctor's office and ordered up a storm of hot food—dosas, idlis, coconut chutney, and warm, milky, sugary coffee. We sat across from one another, beaming.

"Thank you. Thank you for all of your care," I said, humbled by her thoughtfulness. "As if you didn't have enough on your hands." For some reason, this had us falling into a fit of laughter. We laughed for a long, long time, leaving the outside world at bay for a few precious moments.

22

REIMAGINING

*Until we understand what is within, we can't
understand what is without.*

—Anita Moorjani

I RETURNED TO WORK at the foundation after my three-month break with a renewed sense of grounding. The earthquake and the years following set me on a search for a truth so fundamental that I couldn't believe I had made it so far in my life without understanding it. It was like a glacier had been quietly melting and shifting under my feet. I could barely notice the difference from one day to the next, but when I looked back, the transformation was startling, and I realized I had come a long way from where I started.

I had been forced to turn my attention inward, to nurture a respect for the strength and power I held in myself. I had learned in an incredibly roundabout way that in order to help others find their greatness, I had to find my own.

But this hadn't been handed to me, nor had it happened on its own in an isolated vacuum. It had unfolded through a process of healing that involved many, many acts of kindness from others and by listening and seeing, with a new lens, the amazing interplay at work in life in the natural and spiritual worlds. If we sat quiet and still, we could receive gifts from them—energy and wisdom, new and ancient—and it could flow through our fingertips. It could sustain us. We just had to let go, open up, and reach out. It was all there. There was an infinite, limitless source that didn't have a bottom to it, and it belonged to us all.

Understanding this made me able to walk more lightly and see more clearly. It had me thinking long and hard about the work we were trying to do at GoPhil, and why, at times, philanthropy could miss the mark so terribly. Interestingly, there were important epiphanies in the giving world that I was experiencing myself. A shift was taking place, one that would reveal itself across many aspects of our societies, as people shined a light on the unique potential they had to change and heal themselves. And they were recognizing that the best possibilities for their futures could never be simply handed to them; true growth would need to be born from their own visions.

But in the same way that I had been required to undo myself, it was time to dismantle some of the structures that prevented this in the giving world. Historically, answers to poverty have been sought from external sources who evaluated and identified what was lacking—what was not there. The job was then to fill the hole. Donors were seen as the "givers" who had the "answers," and because they held the funding, they held the control in the relationship. This imbalance prevented people and programs from being the creators of their own positive development. These old ways of trying to fix inequality were actually creating more of the same.

Various leaders in the philanthropic community, wise and grounded thinkers like Lynne Twist and Jennifer Lentnor, were pushing back on these outdated practices. They spoke of abundance instead of scarcity, of there being enough for everyone. Philanthropy needed to be about unearthing more of what is already in each of us and less about transactional giving from those who have "more" to people who have "less." Traditional aid had not been successful in driving long-term change because it didn't focus on what was already present in communities that were deemed poor. Within them was a tremendous well of untapped wisdom and potential that needed to be acknowledged. The job was to help what was there to expand.

One particular individual whose work and writings moved me profoundly was Edgar Villanueva, a Native American racial justice activist, philanthropist, and author of *Decolonizing Wealth: Indigenous Wisdom to Heal Divides and Restore Balance*. Edgar carefully exposes the not-so-pretty roots of philanthropy in America, explaining that these resources had been unfairly amassed since colonial times on the backs of indigenous and marginalized people. I had trouble turning the pages—his message was difficult to ingest. I was ashamed of the history of philanthropy which I had wrongly assumed had been based only on pure intentions. Edgar urges us to recognize this unjust legacy as an important part of healing and giving birth to a new system.

His description of the possibilities of doing things differently spoke to my heart.

"... it's about the whole flock. Everyone has the potential to lead, and leadership is about listening and being attuned to everyone else. It's about flexibility. It's about humility. It's about trust. It's about having fun along the way. It is more about holding space for others' brilliance than being the sole source of answers ..."

These words—holding space, the whole flock, trust, and humility—had been my beacons in the night over the past few years. The fun part didn't always come easily, but I was sure it would in due time. When strung together, I thought these words told a powerful new story for ourselves and how we could work together to build a better future. The dialogue spoke to a need to reimagine how we perceived and approached giving, and it cried out for a new language to describe what this could be. It was time to move from limiting terms that put labels and rigid identities on people: the us/them, rich/poor, developed/undeveloped, giver/receiver terms which ultimately reinforced the separation of people. A new language could reflect our reciprocity instead of division. It could represent how our care, our actions for each other, small and large, mirror our interconnection instead of just measuring the impact we were attempting to make.

Injustice and inequities, found not only in the types of places GoPhil worked, but in my own developed countries, represented an illness, a poverty that was ultimately affecting us all. None of us could take ourselves out of what was needed to make it better. We could only get there together, working on ourselves and as one united system, breathing the same air. We all had to show up.

I couldn't help but look at all of this and see the similarities with what I had experienced in myself. Despite what I might have been showing on the outside, I had struggled with a sense of frailty and feeling as if I was not enough. I had felt powerless and insignificant, and I carried guilt in different ways. I had needed a new language. I had looked outside of myself in search of my answers, when all I needed to do was go in and recognize they were already there. My partners had been people who helped me find the tools to uncover this.

A big, fat light bulb was turning on, and it was shedding light far beyond myself. Healing our sick selves and our world would never be about solving, fixing, or finding perfection. Our medicine would be about discovering and helping each other return to who we already are. And that takes work. Sometimes it's ugly, long, hard and humble work that we have to do alone. At other times, we will do it together, helping one another. Either way, it isn't good enough to want to give back without understanding where and how our own guilt, control, and identity show up in the process. When we know what drives us, what motivates us, and what hurts us, we can better understand what we might have to offer. And maybe, it might just flow with less effort or a need for a return. We will be asked to walk into our aches and pain, to stare at them and sit with them, instead of running from them. We will be forced to go to vulnerable places in order to evaluate what has become an ugly word—privilege. But it's what we do with it that will reveal the beauty on the other side of it. My past difficult years had been one big, long lesson in all of this.

One early fall afternoon, I sat and thought about where things were with GoPhil and where it was in its own journey. While the foundation had always been rooted in the values of self-reliance and helping people reach their full potential, it was perhaps time to peel back the layers of our own organization and assess if there were blind spots to be considered in the way we functioned. Were there areas of our own process that needed to be undone? How did privilege show up subtly and not so subtly within our relationships? Did we have diverse voices at our table that allowed us to see and function with the fullest vantage point? Were our partners involved in creating the systems we had developed which aimed to help them?

Luckily, we had all of the right elements at our fingertips to help us navigate this difficult introspection. Anne Elgerd was our board chair, and she had been gently encouraging us to ask ourselves these questions for some time. She worked diligently in helping us identify where there might be control issues imbedded in some of the common practices surrounding the granting of funds. We connected with other foundations and organizations who had undergone similar self-analyses. The Global Fund for Community Foundation had generated a campaign #shiftthepower to shift the control to local programs on the ground who better understood what they needed for themselves. We weren't alone; there were wise advisors to help guide us.

The timing for all of this was serendipitous, as Linda and Tracey and I were ready to step out of our operational leadership roles and make room for new, fresh thinking and ideas at the foundation. We were nearing a decade of focusing a significant amount of our personal time on GoPhil. Change was in the air and while the letting go was scary for each of the co-founders individually, we knew GoPhil was ready for a much broader and inclusive identity.

Our core operational team had grown over the recent years, and we had wise and capable people sharing in the leadership—Emily Bild, Jill Roeder, and Travis Day were ready to carry the space forward, and they were carefully building a global team that was committed to the same.

Something else was happening at GoPhil, one that was most important for its own health and ability to thrive in the future and one that I had been learning in my own life. Ever so slowly, we were beginning to shed the self-sacrificial culture that had been present from the start. Our work had attracted incredibly hard-working, compassionate individuals whose discomfort with the inequity that existed in the world kept them up at night and had them working all-too-long hours. Involvement at GoPhil was very rewarding, but we were exposed on a daily basis to the hardship and difficulty that people faced in regions lacking the basics. We each carried a sense of responsibility that surpassed what each one of us could possibly achieve individually.

Over time, we were seeing the value in tending to ourselves as an organization—that our sustainability would not be found in carrying the weight of the world on our shoulders, nor from sacrifice. As a team, we started to be mindful of each other, ensuring that joy, laughter, and celebration were part of our make-up. We could be warriors in our loyalty to our partners, but we could also be kind to ourselves. While there would always be more to do, we could soften and know that what we were doing was enough. It had taken time, but the terms *play, grace, and clarity* were revealing their messages everywhere I looked.

23

FREE FALLING

There is nothing more important to true growth than realizing that you are not the voice of the mind, you are the one who hears it.

—Michael Singer

THE SUMMER OF 2019, Emma turned twenty-one, and many of our close family members gathered at Mas de Gancel to celebrate. It was an extra special moment as it would be the last summer in the house before moving to Les Agnels at the end of the year. We had wanted to enjoy every moment of our time there and decided to only rent it for three weeks of that summer season. It would be a rare occasion for us to have some fun in our home and pool during the weeks we had typically rented it out to others. And despite knowing we wouldn't be living there for much longer, I started a proper vegetable garden next to the vineyard, something I had dreamed of doing much more of since tending to our dry strip of earth next to our house in California.

It was hard to believe Emma was hitting this big milestone and even harder to grasp letting go of a place where we had made so many memories. But something about the moment just felt right. We had so much to be thankful for. We had survived separating as a family, the kids were all thriving in their own ways, and on the whole, I was feeling better physically.

A few days prior to the family gathering, John and I had popped a bottle of champagne for another unrelated yet important happening. After over a year of trying to establish Provence Life, his new real estate sales and renovation company, he received his "carte professionnelle," giving him the legal right to be involved in real estate transactions in France. Looking back, we could now laugh at the grueling effort it had taken him to get to this point and begin looking forward to helping others build their lives in such a magical region. I could finally take a big, long breath—*I think we have found terra firma.*

The moment was all pretty close to perfect with one exception. Sometime prior to the family gathering, we started to receive a series of letters from the French tax authority. They were looking into how Only Provence, our US-based villa agency, was structured and began to make a case for all sorts of unfounded claims that we were unjustly avoiding the value-added tax that French-based companies were required to pay.

At first, John didn't take it all too seriously, the sums they were asking for were astronomical—ludicrous, in fact. It was par for the course in dealing with the heavy administrative challenges that came alongside living in France, but having found a lifestyle that felt uniquely right for us, the headaches were a trade-off we had agreed to make. For the first few days, the issue seemed to be one that could be ironed out and logically explained, but as time passed, I could see on John's face and in his demeanor that fear was setting in. The what-ifs started to weave their way into his thoughts. In a matter of days, full-on panic had begun to set in.

"Lyd—this is a pretty ugly situation. If they actually prove this crazy case and successfully slap this fine on us, we won't make it. We will have to close Only Provence, and everything I have built over the past fifteen years will be gone." Negative thoughts began to spin out of control, and the domino effect was disastrous. We considered all of the people who either worked for or consulted with our company, which included three couples whom we loved like family, and who logically depended on their incomes. "The kids are not independent. We have heavy bills to pay to support their rent in LA and to pay for Emma's and Izzy's schools. What would we do without an income if we have to close? What would happen to all of that?" We had savings, of course, but we hadn't planned for the worst of financial situations—going ninety miles an hour to a full stop. And then there was the shame in thinking how we would be perceived by others, without any of what we had accomplished to show for ourselves propped up next to us.

Another massive moving piece added to the stress: After all of the moving around, a home was finally in sight for us. Over the past year, we had knocked over one of the old structures at Les Agnels, and our new home was being built, brick by brick. We had been dreaming and planning for this for so long, but if the business failed, we would have to rethink following through on it. Or we would need to consider finishing it and putting it up for sale. And where would we go? Back home? And where was that exactly?

As John worked his way through the various machinations, fear truly took hold and wouldn't let go. His father had left his family when John was seven, and since that moment, he had felt a responsibility that children don't normally take on—aren't meant to take on. Since then, he had vowed to build a solid foundation and care for himself and the people around him. Whether consciously or not, he decided he was going to make things right by investing in the only thing he felt he had full control of—his own confidence and abilities. Success would happen, come hell or high water, with positivity and drive, with sweat equity and determination. And it had. But it had also come from privileges that he had been given from the get-go. He was a white man, good-looking, and well-educated, and there was no doubt this had made navigating life's challenges easier for him than for others.

But in that ugly moment, maybe that was part of what wasn't working, what was crashing. All of these things could only take him so far. As is true for each one of us, true strength is grounded in something more fundamental, and finding it would require a trust in something deeper.

I listened and watched as my strong, capable man became someone I didn't recognize. He stopped sleeping and eating. He stopped making jokes and singing as he had always done while doing the dishes. He woke up at night and gripped his chest in pain as his mind tricked him into believing that he was the sum of a line of successful, accomplished actions.

When the family arrived for Emma's birthday, laughter filled the hallways of Gancel, and a constant train of Aperol Spritzes made their way from the kitchen to the poolside. While the diversion was good, John couldn't hide what was going on. He explained the situation, and each member of the family listened and provided support in their own way. Nick would sit with him, taking in the details of the situation, trying to keep his confidence up. "Dad, you will be fine," he said. "We will be fine. Please don't worry." John had been by his side a million times as he had stood in front of audiences, in front of all the acceptances and the rejections of his career. And now in this moment, there was no option but to do the same. Emma brought her youthful laughter and lightheartedness to the room. He needed that. Her dad would never be anyone but the biggest and the strongest in her eyes. Izzy showed her love quietly, sitting next to John at dinners where everyone was full of happiness and fun, except him. My sister, Helene, sat while he had a watershed moment. They had grown up together and had been there for one another through many of life's harsh turns. My cousin Wendy's husband is a well-known solicitor in London. He was at the ready with referrals to capable lawyers to defend our case. It was amazing to see and feel all of the love and energy that filled the gaps that were empty for John in that difficult moment.

My heart broke seeing him this way. I knew I was powerless to fix what he thought was his responsibility to make right for us all. He had been a rock for me since the day I met him. For years, he had sat patiently as I cried over finding my way to doing something meaningful with my life, yet not knowing where on earth to start. He had left his comfortable, secure life in the US to find what it was that I was sure was out there, but didn't know how to describe it nor where to find. He had helped give birth to so much that had mattered to me in life—my family and GoPhil. He had been the pillar for it all, and now he felt he was in a free-fall, not knowing who would catch him before the ground appeared.

But my past years had taught me much, and I knew he wouldn't find the harsh bottom of that fall. An important process to it all had to be honored. A nugget of something vital was to be found within the drop. I was also learning another critical lesson that was only just beginning to reveal its power. I knew that I couldn't take on his pain, nor fix it. I could only do one thing, and that was to hold space for him while he faced his demon, his earthquake. We would all have them, and if we are brave enough to greet them, we could get beyond them. They needn't define us. They were but voices in our heads. What we are made up of far exceeds these threats. Light can be found through these cracks.

My logical mind worked through losing the money and the homes, perhaps both Mas de Gancel and Les Agnels, but nobody could take what really mattered from us. We would sit together, looking out at the vineyard, and talk about what we did have. Our health, each other, and our loved ones. What flowed between them could never be taken away.

The rest of that summer crept by as slow as molasses. While we had two sets of lawyers on the job, one in France and one in the US, the French tax departments would be shut until the end of the summer. And if anyone is familiar with this region, they know that the French take their weeks off in the summer as seriously as their wine. We had to become comfortable with not knowing what fate would bring. The long, hot weeks gave John time to reflect on his life and his accomplishments. He went through his mental closets, figuring out what needed to stay and what no longer served him. He made calls to people he cared for, saying things that needed to be said. At times this was an I love you, at others it was a thank you, and sometimes it was I'm sorry. I knew he was making progress through this difficult process when he began to sleep through the night and chuckle to himself while doing the dishes.

In the early mornings and evenings, when the air was cool, we would go out into our little vegetable patch and delight from what had grown overnight or during the day. We chatted with our neighbor Patrick, an avid gardener who shared with us all sorts of guidance on how to care for our plants. We were amazed at what could emerge so perfectly from the ground. These small moments over the weeks helped shift the focus off the fear and onto what was more important. More and more I observed as my man opened up and began to trust in something other than himself.

We spent a good deal of time at Les Agnels during those long summer days. At some point, one of us noticed that if we switched the letters of Agnels around, they formed the word "angels." As a believer in angels, I loved that thought. I was also comforted in that it was similar to Los Angeles, and if you added the letter C, it could also form the word Gancel. There was something about the letters that strung together so many vital parts that had made up our lives, but then again, I had always known there was a magic to the place.

In July, the Les Agnels hamlet came alive as the bright purple fields of lavender were harvested, and massive tractors pulling bins of the cut flowers were brought to the distillery located next to our property. We watched as the local men worked together using pitchforks to move the flowers into a vat that would be pressed with a massive, old, heavy tire. The flowers would then begin their long road of slowly transforming into a powerful essence. We stood dumbfounded at both the simplicity and complexity of the process as we took in the air, thick with fragrance.

Our building site changed rapidly on a daily basis; it was amazing to see the evolution from what had been such fragile, vine-covered ruins to a sturdy and strong house. The old, original home that we had hoped to renovate had, unfortunately, been too unstable to build upon. Months prior, it had been pushed over by a bulldozer, its remains forming a massive pile of ancient stone by the side of the country road. We had been devastated at the time, torn apart by the need to demolish a house that had stood the test of time for so long. But we would reuse pieces of what had been there—old wooden beams would become the shelves in my library, and the stones were carefully restacked to create our bedrooms walls.

On the other side of the property stood the facade of the second ancient structure. We learned it was called "Le Marronier," as it faced a big and beautiful chestnut tree. Our talented team of masons had carefully dug out the interior of this side of the ruins and fortified its old stone walls. It now stood completely open to the sky, like so many of the stunning cathedrals I had visited in Guatemala that had been demolished in the earthquakes. Sitting inside the walls of this roofless structure one afternoon, I figured out what I loved most about it not being enclosed; it made me feel I was right where I needed to be, perfectly sandwiched between the magic of the earth and the sky.

Over the months, we had made an amazing discovery on the property. Behind one of the broken walls that had been covered in plant growth and fallen wooden beams was a small, vaulted stone cave. If you placed a ladder from the opening on what would have been its roof, you could climb down and stand inside of it. Apart from this hole in its roof, it was amazingly intact. The walls were built perfectly with gorgeous stones, and they arched as they made their way to the ceiling. A wall at the end of the room divided the space. We noticed a small section that could have been used to store liquid. "It must have been a cistern for water or for where they made wine," John said one day. "Why don't we make it a wine cellar!"

But something was uniquely special about this ancient room that I couldn't put my finger on. A peace was inside of it that I had only found in sacred places—in places of worship. Specks of light found their way through the broken part of the roof, and small wildflowers had crept in, moving softly in the wind.

"No," I said. "It feels more like a chapel." John looked at me with a furrowed brow and a smirk on his face as if he was ready to make a joke. But he knew I was serious.

Eventually, our masons carefully uncovered a natural opening to the room from the outside, an elegant arched doorway that must have existed from the start. We now could enter the chapel from the heart of the ruins. On our visits to Agnels, I found myself drawn to this hidden room more and more. It had become a sanctuary of sorts and reminded me of the crumbled cave-like ruins of the monastery in Antigua, Guatemala, where Hermano Pedro had lived. I learned later that he was both a gifted mason as well as a gardener. It made me wonder about the connection between these two activities, both of which could seem like simple jobs on the surface, yet I was pretty sure held deeper purposes. At times I meditated in my chapel, but just sitting inside felt equally as restful. I would look at the pile of stones that had fallen through the opening, allowing the fading sun to cast beautiful, bright shadows across the dirt floor.

In the coming weeks, we would learn more about this special cave. John was giving a tour of the property to Bernadette and Maurice Agnel. They had been the owners of the property and had gifted it to their daughter Julie, whom we had ultimately bought it from. When they neared the chapel, Bernadette turned to John and said "Je peux t'avouer quelque choses (*Can I admit something to you?*)"

They had been a little nervous in sharing the story, as they thought it might make us uncomfortable. Bernadette then recounted that a priest had been buried on the property, and she believed it to be in the location of our so-called chapel. John went silent for a moment, surprised at the connection between the story and what had become a sanctuary. Maurice's parents still lived in the hamlet; they were nearing a hundred years old—they would know for sure, they said. The following week, we paid a visit to the older Agnel couple. We spent hours in their kitchen listening to stories of life in the hamlet and how they had lived entirely off the land. When the moment felt right, I asked Madame Agnel if there was indeed a priest who had been buried on our property.

"Oui," she said without hesitation, and she then described the exact location of our chapel.

We felt incredibly grateful for being accepted into the hamlet. Foreigners with their new ideas and different ways of life were not always welcomed so warmly. People who came in and pushed over ancient stone homes to rebuild new ones were not always liked. But our neighbors had an open and positive spirit, and they were thrilled to see what had stood uncared for change into something new. Over time, we were brought into their houses, and one by one, they opened up to us, sharing their homemade vin d'orange and their life stories. We learned about lavender and cherry harvesting and warned about the *sanglier* (wild boar) that roamed the trails.

On our drives back to Mas de Gancel, we would sometimes worry and talk about the fact that we might not see the day when we could actually live in Les Agnels, but as time went on, we let that go, little by little. The experience was so rich, so full, that it took over the space that fear had held.

24

WAITING

The wound is the place where the Light enters you."

—Rumi

I AWOKE ABRUPTLY from an unsettling dream. I had been walking around an orphanage, and looking into a room, I set my eyes on a child. She was about two years old and visibly frail. She had a mark on her neck, somewhat like Isabelle, who also has a birthmark on the right side of her neck. The child had blond, scruffy hair and was wearing faded pajamas with pink spots. John was with me, and we had been in the room with this child for some time yet were on our way out, leaving for some reason. We told the caretakers that we would come back a few weeks later.

The dream then fast-forwarded to our return. We had been gone for what felt like a very long time. When we entered the orphanage, the caretaker said that the young girl had been in mourning, waiting quietly for our return, not showing interest in playing or in eating much at all. When we approached her, she was sitting on the floor in front of a row of books. Turning, she looked up at us. Her relief was apparent, and I bent down and took her into my arms. This was a child I knew very, very well, a knowing that ran into the core of my being. It was as if she had been waiting for us for a lifetime and as though she would continue to wait for yet another one, if she had to.

In the moment, it was a haunting dream, and I fumbled for my little purple notebook to scribble down the details—I knew they would fade as daily life worked its way into my mind. For weeks I thought of the dream and wondered who she was. *Was she the face of so many children I had seen over the years, living in institutions, patiently yet sadly waiting to be picked up, waiting to be saved?*

No, I thought. I knew deep down that she wasn't asking to be saved. This girl was waiting for something she knew belonged to her. She was waiting to go home.

I wondered if she was a reflection of the belonging that we were all searching for—of Izzy longing for her Chinese mother, of my friend Sam who deserved a safe home, of the hundreds of children I had witnessed who had been so unfairly separated from their families. I thought of the faces of the girls in Dhulikhel and the woman who had been left to die on the streets of Kolkata.

And then there was yet another question—*Was this little girl me?* My mind wandered to my own struggle with finding what home meant. *Why had it been so hard to find it?*

But something told me she was waiting to return to a place that went beyond the four walls of what I had been looking for. For years, I had been looking for a physical place, but maybe what

I was searching for, the real home, wasn't a place at all. Maybe it had everything to do with finding our way back to a place inside ourselves that had always been there. Over time, as I thought back on the dream, it slowly became deeply reassuring.

As the year came to a close, we prepared to move into Les Agnels. I would only have a couple of short weeks to unpack our container that had been shipped from Los Angeles and somehow get a Christmas tree up before the kids arrived. But before even opening the boxes, I walked out to the chapel in the cold December wind with an armful of candles. I placed them all around the room, tucking them into little nooks where rocks had fallen from the walls. Afterward, I placed a small stone statue of Mary under the archway of the entrance.

As the kids' arrival dates approached, I was nervous, afraid that they would feel the loss of Mas de Gancel, their childhood home. I feared they would sense, as I had for so much of my life, untethered from roots. John and I spent days opening boxes, arranging our things, not quite knowing what to say. Les Agnels was surreal, something we had created together. It felt too good to be true, and somewhere, we knew it just might be. We knew all too well the reality of our tenuous business situation and the potential ramifications of not being able to hold onto it.

The kids tumbled in, one after the other—Nick ragged from a marathon session in Iceland where he had been filming his upcoming music video, and Emma a week later, jet-lagged and exhausted from final exams in fashion design school. Isabelle returned from boarding school in Aix, thrilled to have the family reunited and all in one place. To my relief, all three were giddy about the new house and bonded instantly with the views and the surrounding trails. We spent evenings by the fire with good food and wine, watching movies and playing Monopoly. On New Year's Eve, we lit incense and candles in the chapel and star-gazed under thick blankets. Various dogs from the hamlet joined us, and we couldn't have been happier. I could feel myself attempting to cling to the moment, to never let it end, but I knew better. Instead, I captured it in my heart and let it go.

25

FINDING LIGHT

She is the Divine Essence that lives within all beings.
Her domain is the field of life, for she gives to all beings
the sustenance that is needed for life.

—Devi Prayer

IN EARLY 2020, I traveled to India to see Anuradha and to visit Dr. Haldvedekar once more. While I was feeling better, I still experienced bouts of deep body pain. The Ayurvedic practices and the herbs had soothing effects on my system, and I wanted to delve deeper into the study of the earth's natural healing properties.

During my trip, I underwent panchakarma, a series of Ayurvedic cleansing and detoxifying rituals. My mornings would entail several hours at the doctor's small clinic where I would be rubbed with carefully selected oils, then placed in an aluminum steam box to allow them to be infused into my skin. I took handfuls of herbs at various times of the day, all prepared in the doctor's home kitchen. Some days I laid down on a wooden table where a large metal funnel slowly dripped warm, herb-scented oil onto my forehead. Afterward, I would wait by the side of the road for my ride back to the hotel, the typically loud and jarring Indian street noises strangely muted by my treatments. I would stumble back to my room, oily, warm, and feeling slightly drunk.

Sometime during the panchakarma process, I awoke in the middle of the night with an urgent need to find Sam, my childhood friend that I had lived next door to in Ottawa. After years of thinking and worrying about her, I immediately found her on Facebook. I reached out without hesitating, praying she would respond. Within seconds, I saw the three dots indicating she was writing back. I could barely breathe as I waited for her reply. In a series of heartfelt exchanges, we spoke honestly, and I shared with her everything I had felt for so long. I gently unloaded all of the shame I had been carrying for events I would not allow myself to remember. I told her how much I cared for her, and that I was sorry for running away.

Just like that, in a matter of thirty minutes, I released a heavy blanket of darkness that I had been carrying with me for over forty years. It was hard to fathom, and I was distinctly aware of a massive release, maybe one of the most significant in my life. But I also allowed myself to hold onto a few remaining threads. Somehow the ugliness of the situation had also sparked a fire in me to fight for others in similar situations, and that task had required me to find a force within I didn't know I had. Tucked into my hotel bed in that moment, my laptop on my knees and tears streaming down my face, I finally acknowledged and honored this, letting it replace the space that shame had taken up in me for so long.

I learned through later exchanges with Sam that her life had not been easy but that she had a daughter who brought her great joy. Some of the fondest memories of her childhood were of riding tricycles on her driveway with me.

It was dark when I drove home from the airport from that trip back into the Luberon hills, up the winding lanes and into the rocky dirt road of Les Agnels hamlet. As I got out of the car, a gentle, cool breeze swept across my tired traveled body. I turned to see the white cap of Mont Ventoux, bright and visible, even at this late hour, in the distance. The shadowy figure of my man bounded up the steps to my car, wearing the worn leather Doc Martens boots he had worn for nearly fifteen years. My heart skipped a beat as I tucked into his arms. "Hey babe," he said happily, kissing the top of my head. "You smell like India!" he said chuckling. He had bounced back to his normal self again, full of dreams and endless optimism.

The fire was lit, and I fell into the couch. I had returned home, as I had with each trip, different. And unbeknownst to me, it would be the last long-haul flight I would take for a long time. The world was on the brink of an epic transformation and two months later, COVID-19 spread like wildfire, destabilizing an already fragile system. Strangely, life for everyone, as we had each known it, would change at the same time.

The only choice was to surrender to the situation and focus on what we had in front of us. Isabelle came home from school, and Provence's beautiful, vibrant region of markets and cafés closed down. Our villa rental company, alongside so many other businesses across the world, came to a grinding halt. Had John not been faced with the fear of losing it all the summer before, he might have lost his footing. He was deeply concerned as he filled out the application for the relief loans being offered, worried for the families who depended on Only Provence for their livelihoods, but he also believed there was more to it than what the moment was presenting in the short term. We had to ride out the storm and accept the reality of not knowing what the future would bring.

As each day passed, the implications of the situation revealed themselves further, one after the other. I worried about our parents on the other side of the ocean who were all reaching a certain age—being so far away, there was no way to help them. I struggled with being physically cut off from Nick and Emma. They hunkered down in their LA apartments, while riots and fires ravaged the city alongside the spreading virus. I felt like my mother arms had been tied around my body with thick rope.

Difficult news came in from all of the programs we were involved with at GoPhil. While the virus took longer to infiltrate some of their regions, vulnerable communities felt the brutal blow of a loss of income right away. It was as if a nightmare had become a reality. Hunger took hold, and their pleas for help ran shockwaves through our organization. We responded in the only way we knew how. We promised to stand by them, to make every effort we could to find resources for them.

As our borders and homes became even more divided and separated, the pandemic seemed to highlight the inequities that had long needed attention. For too long, injustice had been starving certain people from their natural right to thrive, and now violence and anger were seeping through the pores of a toxic, unwell system.

The Black Lives Matter movement took center stage, and people far and wide began to wake up to the notion that we each held a power to act, and it could no longer be wasted. Privilege had shifted from an opportunity to work on behalf of a whole, to one of misuse and abuse of what had never been owned by anyone in the first place. It made me think back to what Julio shared at the clinic in Guatemala—we needed to return to what indigenous cultures had always known. Everything is interconnected. If there is illness or a lack of life force in one area, it will weaken the whole system.

On a sunny spring morning, John and I went out to a patch of empty soil in front of the house next to the cherry grove—the special place we had thought we might put a long and elegant swimming pool. Instead, we turned over the heavy, rich soil and carved out four thick rows that would make up our vegetable garden. We were a little unsure of the location—perhaps there would be too much direct sun during the searing summer afternoons. Would the wind blow too hard from the north? We finally threw caution to the wind and just dug in, pulling up thick, old weeds and removing the rocks from the soil. For weeks I sowed seeds in my laundry room—tomatoes, butternut squash, eggplant, watermelon, and peppers. In the mornings, I would check in on them before I made my coffee, seeing how they had fared through the night.

With not much else to focus on, I became consumed with new growth under our roof. When the days warmed enough to be sure that frost was no longer a threat, I carefully transplanted my baby plants to the empty beds, watching vigil as they settled into their new home.

As the weeks slipped by, I spent a lot of time in what we referred to lovingly as the "patch." The dogs would follow me out, tucking themselves into the warm, earthy soil to take in the sun at my feet while I weeded and pruned. We had taken in a second dog, Choupie, who had needed a new home the previous spring. She was a playful white terrier with deep brown eyes. Life seemed less complicated in the patch. It was easy to feel good out there, like playing in a sandpit, and I was drawn to it more and more. It was a calling that I now recognized well—one that wasn't to be ignored. My patch was like a long finger, motioning me to come. She had things to teach, metaphors to bring into our broader lives.

Like life, nothing stayed the same from one day to the next; I was in awe of the changes each and every day. The vegetables grew in their own time, sometimes taking much longer than I ever expected for them to reach their peak harvest moments. The tomatoes sprouted and formed, fast and furiously, as did the zucchini and squashes, stretching their way down the stone wall, dangling over the side like children on a swing. The peppers grew steadily yet what felt like slowly over the course of four months. This seemed like an eternity in the moment, but I could feel the celebration in the air as the right day to pick some arrived, and in that precious moment, it didn't feel a minute too early or a second too late.

Amazingly though, I never had to worry about my role in this, an ever-changing landscape. All I had to do was show up and be attentive, and I would be put to use. The plants weren't shy in knowing or expressing what they required. They knew how they needed to be nurtured; they wilted or reached for the sky accordingly. Some didn't make it. I observed, carefully letting them take their own lead and do what felt natural. It was an intricate interplay of giving and receiving that became indistinguishable. At times it reminded me of being at Mother Teresa's house. Nobody was there to measure who was doing what and whether it was enough.

In the long, quiet days of lockdown, I finally began to write in earnest about all that had transpired in the past five years, since the day the walls came down in Kathmandu.

The words tumbled out easily across the pages as I revisited the fears, the pain, and the joy that had needed to be sorted through. I carefully decided which ones to let go of entirely and which ones to bring with me. I also thought of things yet undone, like the girls home in Dhulikhel, which I kept wrapped up safely inside my heart. *Some things demand more time and patience. I will never give up hope that they find their way home.*

My mind returned to the incense-filled room in California when Tauheedah had warned me something was missing from the end of my first book. She had been right, so very right. But what had happened since then had been a slow, unexpected journey of another sort, one that required digging into the soil of what existed on the interior. It had taken some weeding, but what I found far exceeded what I ever could have imagined. I discovered that perfection resided deep inside each one of us. My job had never been to control any of what life presented, or to try and make right what was wrong out there. The task, at the end of the day, was much less complex than that. It was a daily one, without a beginning or an end, and one in which health would never be a destination to arrive at, nor true home a place that held a roof. It was about accessing the light that exists within us, and helping others do the same. For we are just as much a part of each other's story as we are a part of our own. We are inextricably connected, sharing an energy that sustains us all. Our own healing and that of our world can only be found when we act as one. Playing in our light was all that had ever been asked of us, and the craziest thing was that it had always been there from the start. On a dark, cool night on the terrace, with the wind in my hair, I felt freer than ever before. Looking out across the vast valley with the twinkling lights of the town of Apt below, I had found home.

GOPHILANTHROPIC
IN GRATITUDE

SO MUCH OF MY LIFE LEARNING has come from my experience in being a part of this dynamic working family. It has been rich in all the important ways. Words could never express the joy and love that I have experienced working alongside all of our partners' programs across the globe—we now know who does the heavy lifting out there.

I would like to take a moment to thank those who have dedicated so much of themselves to the inner workings of GoPhil. Thank you to co-founders Linda DeWolf and Tracey Morrell, two incredibly strong and passionate women who carefully helped to plant the seed of what later grew into a tree that many would help nurture. Your dedication and tireless efforts are etched into the foundation of this special organization. Thank you to Anne Elgerd, my soul sister; you opened my eyes to things I could not yet see for myself. Thank you to Emily Bild, who captures what it means to listen fully in working alongside our courageous partners, and to Jill Roeder, whose deep sensitivities and care for marginalized people is evident in her unwavering daily march. To Travis Day, thank you for gently and compassionately ensuring that the voices from our partner programs are heard far and wide and for holding the sacred, delicate space needed to allow the magic of connecting in person. To Mae Ardon, Mehdeen Abbasi, Corinne Yank, Kevin Rhodes and Gemma Marshall, thank you for helping GoPhil expand its reach even further. None of the work at the foundation could be possible without our Board of Directors, dedicated volunteers, Founder Circle, and community members, who keep it nourished in every way, each day.

I am deeply grateful to Allegra Mangione, Helene O'connor and Pascal Fautrat, who offered significant feedback as the manuscript took shape.

The list is far too long to thank each and every person who has been a part of the journey—you know who you are. Thank you for your belief and for your kindness. It matters.

ABOUT THE AUTHOR

IN 2000, LYDIA DEAN LEFT a successful career in Orlando, Florida, to explore the world with her husband and young children. Settling down in the south of France, they found joy in leading a simpler life while reconnecting with their childhood dreams. During their years outside the US, Lydia traveled extensively to areas lacking access to education and opportunity. Motivated by the simple ideal that small personal actions can make a difference, she and her family returned to the US in 2007 and launched GoPhilanthropic Travel—a social enterprise that engages travelers with the lesser-known humanitarians of the world. In 2011, Lydia co-founded GoPhilanthropic Foundation, a nonprofit organization that collaborates in expanding the potential that resides at the grassroots

In 2015 she published *Jumping the Picket Fence*, an inspirational mixture of travel memoir, soul searching, and nonprofit building. Her second book, *Light Through the Cracks*, was released in 2021. Her story, both raw and relevant, explores how our own personal healing directly relates to our ability to make a difference in the world at large. Lydia currently resides in Provence, France.

Made in the USA
Middletown, DE
21 February 2021